Penmark Past

MAUREEN BULLOWS

First published 1995 by
D. Brown & Sons Ltd,
Cowbridge and Bridgend, South Wales

Reprinted 2000

Produced and published
on behalf of the author by
Robert Boyd Publications
260 Colwell Drive
Witney, Oxfordshire OX8 7LW

ISBN: 1 899536 58 2

© Maureen Bullows

Printed and bound at the Alden Press, Oxford

CONTENTS

Foreword	v
Introduction	vii
Penmark Parish	1
Parish Church	3
Nonconformists & Catholics	13
Charities	17
The Vestry	21
Parish Council	21
Allotments	23
Housing and Sanitation	25
Footpaths and Highways	27
Water	29
Lighting and Electricity	31
Social Events	33
War Activities	37
The School	39
Health	53
Police Force	55
Fire Service	59
Post and Telephone	59
Shops, Pubs and People	61
Farming	65
Development of Transport	69
People and Houses	71
Occupations	71
Conclusion	73
Incumbents	75
Parish Councillors	77
Teachers	79

ILLUSTRATIONS

Fonmon Castle *(above Foreword)*
1. O.S Map 1879
2. Team of horses mowing hay c.1900
3. Kenson Bridge c.1930
4. St. Mary's Church, 1995 showing cross.
5. Penmark Main Street c.1935 showing Post Office.
6. Penmark Main Street c.1935 showing Chapel.
7. Church register burial 1895.
8. Church register baptism 1895.
9. Sefton Cottage c.1900 – named in Blackton Charity.
10. Jeremia and Mary Murphy outside Sefton Cottage.
11. Will of William Jones of Blackton 1713.
12. Charity distribution 1864.
13. Post Office & Cottages c.1940, David Robert's impression.
14. Penmark Main Street c1935 showing Six Bells.
15. Penmark Post Office c.1925 possibly Mr. & Mrs. Thomas.
16. Pleasant Harbour.
17. Newspaper account of life without water 1934.
18. Penmark Pump c.1928.
19. Penmark Pump 1935.
20. Rose and Crown c.1900.
21. The Hunt c.1938.
22. Fonmon School c.1890.
23. Penmark School Pupils 1897.
24. Penmark School Pupils 1927.
25. Miss Thomas at Higher End 1930's.
26. The Cottage c.1925 with village children.
27. School certificate – Fanny Prosser 1896.
28. Group of children outside the school possibly VE celebrations.
29. Auction 1917 – homes of policeman and headmaster.
30. Policeman c.1856 (kind permission of Bridgend Police Museum).
31. Trade Directory 1891.
32. Auction 1959.
33. Villagers watching the hunt.
34. Wheelwright and apprentice c.1920.
35. Preparing for the show c.1900.
36. Auction 1917.
37. Aberthaw Station.
38. Census 1891 (Crown copyright permission of H.M.S.O.).
39. Bowen brothers outside Penmark Farm c.1890.
40. Penmark vicarage c.1900.
41. The Six Bells.
42. The Six Bells.
43. George Hutching school master 1859.

Fonmon Castle

FOREWORD

My family have been living in the Parish of Penmark for almost exactly 350 years. Despite the wealth of anecdote and archive accumulated over this period. I have been amazed at the vast range of facts and figures that Maureen Bullows has managed to unearth, of which I for one am woefully ignorant.

    I am delighted to recommend this book to anyone wishing to discover the history of the place and people of Penmark and its surroundings.

                      Sir Brooke Boothby

Fonmon Castle
November, 1995

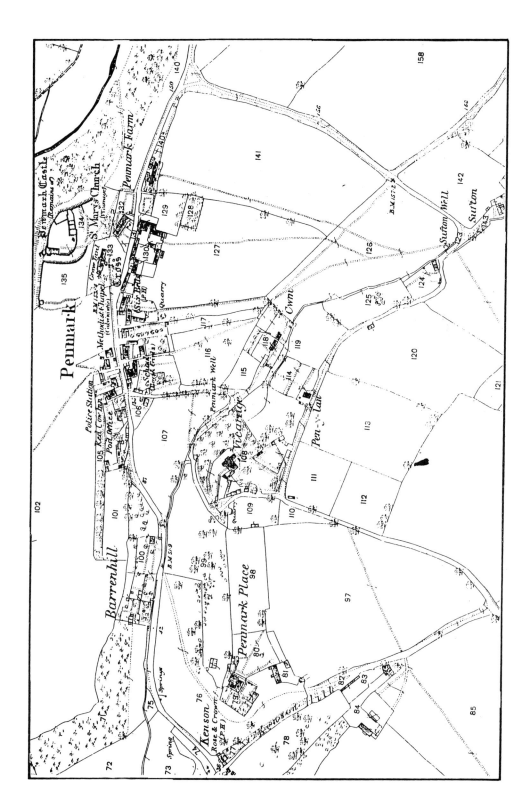

INTRODUCTION

In 1993 whilst decorating the Penmark Village Centre, someone noticed the date 1895 high up on the outside wall. The assumption was that this indicated the date when the school was founded and a history ought to be compiled for the centenary. It soon became apparent that this date actually represented extensive alterations to the building but I decided to continue with my research. In this "centenary" year I have produced a book dealing with the life and people of the parish since 1850.

My thanks are extended to the following for allowing me access to papers and photographs relating to Penmark Parish, D. Roberts, D Williams, I. Hopkins, S. Hardy, N. Lyons, A. Reese, A. Radcliffe, P. Lewis, P. & J. Davies, M. Board, K. Chapman, Miss Murphy, H. Pollard, S. Pare. D. Hoddle, R. & T. Fuller, T. Clemett, A. Mills, J. Daley, S. Brock, G. Jenkins.

Bridgend Police Museum,
Glamorgan Record Office,
Barry Library,
Cardiff Library,
Barry Council,
Post Office Archives.

A special word of thanks is extended to Toni McKerrow for her help and encouragement and to my husband for his help with the text.

Sources
Glamorgan Record Office - Church registers, electors lists, Fonmon papers, school log books, council minutes.
Cardiff library - Western Mail, Charity commissioners reports, trade directories, census returns, St Peter's chair, maps.

2. *Team of horses mowing hay c.1900*

PENMARK PARISH

Penmark parish is in the county of South Glamorgan. It is mentioned in Archaeologia Cambrensis in 1861 as follows:

> "The parish of Penmark lies in the south west corner of the Hundred of Dinas Powys, upon the sea and its landward boundaries are St. Athan's, Llancarvan, Wenvoe, Merthyr-Dovan, Barry and Porthkerry. It is about four miles long from east to west by two miles broad from North to South. The Parish of Penmark contained anciently the villages of Aberthaw, Bourton, Cwm, Fonmon, Fontegarry, Nurston, Rhoose, Treduchan, and Penmark. In 1861, there was a total of five houses at Bourton and Nurston and one farmhouse and two cottages at Treduchan."
>
> "The parish extends to 3235 acres of which 212 are woodland and the remainder equally divided between arable land and pasture; 160 acres are water, including the shore between high and low water mark. There is no common land and the Parish appears always to have been enclosed. The seaboard exclusive of Porthkerry is 2650 yards in length wholly lias cliff. Its western limit is the Tawe river, where it shares in the small harbour of Aberthaw."
>
> "The surface of Penmark is undulatory and though it contains no remarkable hills, its general level is from 80 to 150 feet above the sea and it is intersected by several deep coombes, opening chiefly upon the brook which flowing from Wenvoe and Duffryn, receives a tributary from Llancarvan and from that junction to the Tawe river, traversing an aluvial flat, bears the name of the Kenson. The soil of Penmark is a strong loam, occasionally approaching to clay. It is but very moderately thick and rests upon lias limestone, here disposed in horizontal beds, which form the sea cliff and the floor of the shore."

Penmark village street runs east to west parallel to Weycock river, then dips sharply to the Kenson river which flows into the Bristol channel at Aberthaw. This river forms the boundary between the parishes of Penmark and Llancarfan and the bridge over it was a favourite "battleground" for the youths of the two villages. The houses are mainly situated along this street and many still retain their crofts - long thin strips of land of about an acre dating from the medieval field system.

Penmark parish comprises the manors of Fonmon, Penmark Place (formerly Odyn's Fee) and Penmark. The manor of Fonmon was granted to Sir John St. John by Robert Fitzhamon, a Norman Conqueror. It remained in the possession of his family until 1656 when it was sold under a decree of the Court of Chancery to pay debts of the Earl of Bolingbroke. It was bought by Colonel Philip Jones, a trusted counsellor and friend of Oliver Cromwell, and his descendants have lived there to this day.

Odyn's Fee contains Penmark Place and was the smallest of the three manors. It was owned by the family of Sir Peter le Sore, followed by the Bawdrips from Somerset. In 1615 it was acquired by Sir Edward Lewis of Van, a Sheriff of Glamorgan, and later by Sir Charles Kemeys Tynte. The present owners, the Radcliffe family, acquired the property in 1916.

3. Kenson Bridge c.1930

The manor of Penmark was granted to Sir Gilbert Umfreville. He had built the castle - in ruins for many centuries - soon after the Norman Conquest. It is situated in a commanding position at the top of a steep bank overlooking the Weycock river. It remained in the possession of the Umfrevilles until the reign of Edward III, at which time Sir John St. John of Fonmon married Elizabeth, daughter and co-heiress of Sir Henry Umfreville.

PARISH CHURCH

The parish church of St Mary, which lies at the eastern end of the village, is one of the largest in the Vale of Glamorgan. It dates from the 12th century and its patrons have included the Dean and Chapter of Gloucester, as well as the Dean and Chapter of Llandaff. John Wesley preached from the Jacobean pulpit on Saturday 26th July 1777, at the age of 74 years, on one of his many visits to the Vale. On these occasions, he usually stayed at Fonmon Castle as a guest of the Jones family. The church building comprises a chancel, nave, south porch and western tower open to the nave and containing six bells. The chancel arch is Norman, with numerous mouldings and carvings. The south side of the nave includes an original 13th century window and the font is from that period. Perpendicular style windows were introduced when the south wall was rebuilt in about 1800. The east window was introduced to the building in about 1860. Restoration of the church was carried out in 1893 by J.S. Shepton of Penarth from plans and specifications of Messrs Seddon and Carter, architects of Cardiff.

The vestry meeting decided it was desirable that steps should be taken towards reseating the parish church and the restoration of the bells. The vicar called a meeting of the parishioners in furtherance of this object at which he informed them that over £250 had been collected towards the repairs and improvement of the church and that a meeting would be held as soon as Mr O.H.Jones, the churchwarden, returned from the continent, after which part of the work would be proceeded with without delay. The total cost of the work proposed would be about £650. The restoration was confined to a thorough structural repair of the tower and re flooring and reseating of the nave and chancel. When relaying the floors care was taken to preserve the monumental tablets, even though the sanctuary floor was raised.

The seats of the nave were in oak and of a neat, plain design with provision made for extra accommodation by means of chairs. The chancel benches and altar table, also in oak, were richly carved by Mr Clark of Llandaff. A ringing gallery was introduced and the space beneath enclosed to form a vestry. Plaster was stripped from part of the barrel roof to expose the principal rafters and the main braces. A stone staircase was found leading to the former rood loft in the north wall and this was preserved. The church was reopened for worship after restoration by Rt. Reverend Dr. Richard Lewis, Bishop of Llandaff on Wednesday 20 June 1894. The Bishop and other clergy were given lunch in the schoolroom, prepared by the ladies of the church.

The ring of six bells was originally cast in 1721 by Abraham Rudhall of Gloucester. During the mid 19th century the bell ringers of Penmark and Coity vied with each other to make their bells ring louder than the other. Penmark struck the bells with sledgehammers taken from a nearby smithy, cracking three of them as a result. In 1899

4. *St. Mary's Church, 1995 showing cross.*

three bells, the second, fourth and tenor were recast by Carr of Smethwick with their original inscriptions. They were rehung in new iron frames in place of the old oak beams at the expense of David Thomas Alexander of Dinas Powis in memory of his parents and sister whose names appear on the bells. His father, John, was a churchwarden for 33 years and much respected in the village in which he had lived for almost sixty years. The third bell was rehung in 1976 by White's of Appleton in memory of Dr.Colin McKerrow, a local ringer who lived at Gileston House, previously the Red Cow public house. The inscriptions on the bells are:-

Treble.   GOD SAVE THE CHURCH AND KING A R 1721.

No 2   OLIVER ST. JOHN
RESTORED 1899 IN MEMORIAM JOHN ALEXANDER
RESTORED BY CHARLES CARR LTD.
SMETHWICK.

No 3   ABR. RUDHALL CAST US ALL 1721

No 4   MR. RICH'D GREGORY VICAR A R 1721.
RESTORED 1899 IN MEMORIAM MARY ALEXANDER
RESTORED BY CHARLES CARR LTD.
SMETHWICK.

No 5   PEACE AND GOOD NEIGHBOURHOOD A R 1721

Tenor   THO: LOVE. THO: JAY (CHURCH WARDENS) 1721
RESTORED 1899 IN MEMORIAM
MARGARET ALEXANDER
RESTORED BY CHARLES CARR LTD.
SMETHWICK.

Penmark St Mary's tower was affiliated to the Diocesan Association of Change Ringers at their midsummers meeting on 1 July 1899. An instructor would be sent free of charge if the tower became affiliated and the ringers paid the annual subscription of 1s. 6d. per member. Penmark was the chosen venue for the next quarterly meeting on Boxing Day of that year.

A stained glass window was erected in 1899 in memory of Sarah, the wife of Dr George Neale JP of Barry, and her sister, Maria (both daughters of Thomas Mathews of Fontygary) who attended Penmark church. The Lord Bishop of Llandaff dedicated the peal of bells and unveiled the new stained glass window at a service in the church on 14 March 1899. So important an occasion was it that the school was closed for three days and used on the 14th for a public luncheon and tea. The Western Mail records scenes of festivity and rejoicing as the Lord Bishop, assisted by a large number of clergy and a congregation of parishioners and residents of the neighbourhood, dedicated the window and recast bells. "The service was musically rendered by the choir led by the energetic and popular vicar, the Reverend Edward Morgan, who in conjunction with his wardens, Messrs O.H.Jones and William Alexander, had done

5. *Penmark Main Street c.1935 showing Post Office.*

much to add to the beauty and comfort of the church to improve the services. More needs to be done to complete the requirements of the church and it is to be hoped that an effort will soon be made or some kind donor found to replace the harmonium by an organ, a want much felt by the increasing congregation and by the vicar." This remark passed unnoticed as it was 1945 before Mr Ernest Harbottle, the son of the first Parish Clerk, presented the church with an organ.

Among many memorials and embellishments in the church there is a marble tablet commemorating Reverend Henry Jones M.A., "the benevolent and faithful vicar of the parish for twelve years from 1783 to 1794" and a plain memorial to Catherine St. John (1672), wife of William St John of Highlight. There are three brass lozenges to the memory of Ann Kemmeys, daughter of Edward Kemmeys (1671), Catherine St John (1672) and Sir Thomas Lewis (1669), which have inscriptions copied from tombstones which were either broken or covered up when the church was restored. On the north wall of the chancel are two alabaster monuments to members of the Lewis family who lived at Penmark Place. This family presented to the church a silver alms dish and later a chalice and flagon, hallmarked 1708.

Reverend John Thomas Casberd was vicar of Penmark from 1799 - 1843 and also vicar of Llantwit Major and Llysworney and Canon of Llandaff and Wells. He married Maria Charlotte, eldest daughter of Robert Jones of Fonmon Castle (1738-93). He was a generous benefactor to St John's College Oxford and the college restored his mural and vault adjoining the south porch in 1973.

In the north wall there is a large four-light perpendicular window inserted about 1860 and a two-light window in stained glass. The latter depicts coats of arms and shields of Boteler and displays the Boteler motto - "Do not for to repent". It is a memorial to Robert Boteler of Llandough Castle (d 1866), and his wife Mary Anne Boteler (d 1866) daughter of the Reverend Casberd. Husband and wife died within days of each other and were buried on the same day in the family vault.

There are various memorials to members of the Kemys, Savours, Hopkins and Spencer families (whose names recur throughout the parish registers) and one to five men of the parish who gave their lives in the 1914-18 war. The lectern commemorates Reverend Frederick Charles Wood. The brass cross and candlesticks came from the church of St Peter in Aberthaw.

There are mural monuments to many of the Jones family of Fonmon Castle. There is one to Robert Jones of Fonmon Castle (1681-1715), who was Member of Parliament for Glamorgan in the last parliament of Queen Anne and the first of George I, the monument links him through his forebears to Caradoc Vraychvas, Prince of Wales. There is a monument to Robert Jones (1773 - 1834) and his brother Major-General Oliver Jones (d 1815) which was erected by Robert Oliver Jones (1811-86); a painted stone medal at the base of the monument is a replica of a gold medal awarded to the Major General who fought with Sir John Moore in the Peninsular War.

Others were erected to Alicia, second daughter of Evan Thomas, Llwynmadoc, Breconshire (and Old Sully House) (d 1851) first wife of Robert Oliver Jones, Maria Antonia Jones (d 1869) second wife of Major General Oliver Jones and mother of Robert Oliver Jones and Rosa Antonia Cholmely, Rear Admiral Oliver John Jones (d 1878) second son of Major General Oliver Jones and his second wife Maria Antonia. Another was erected to Robert Oliver Jones (d 1886) eldest son of Major General Oliver Jones and Maria Antonia. He was Chairman of Glamorgan Quarter Sessions for 22

6. *Penmark Main Street c.1935 showing Chapel.*

years. He married first Alicia daughter of Evan Thomas of Llwynmadoc, and secondly Sarah Elizabeth daughter of John Bruce Pryce of Dyffryn.

On the outside of the south wall of the church is a mass or scratch dial used in the Middle Ages to indicate the times of the services, but which was later developed to mark the hours of the day.

In the churchyard, the stocks, which were under one of three yew trees, have long since disappeared. However, there still remains a large cross, the steps of which are medieval, but the shaft and cross are late 19th century. The inscription on the socket stone records that "in 1888 these ancient steps were by subscription restored and the cross set therein, the old cross having been there from a date beyond living memory."

The imposing vicarage (used as such until 1970) was built about 1830. The site of the previous one is marked on the first ordnance map (1879) as being to the north east of the church. An early incumbent of the new vicarage was Charles Wood, the son of a Manchester gentleman, who became vicar in 1843. He had matriculated at the age of 15, before going to Pembroke College, Oxford, and spent the first ten years of his ministry in Gloucestershire before moving to Penmark which was in the gift of the Dean and Chapter of Gloucester. He died in office in 1891, after nearly 50 years in the village. His obituary states:

> "he was one of the very few old type of clergymen to be found in the district, was possessed of a most gentlemanly bearing and was highly respected not only in his own parish but also by friends and acquaintances."

He was followed by Edward Morgan, a Cambridge graduate, who came to Penmark after serving seven years in Llanishen and Cardiff. From Penmark he moved to Trevethin, progressing to Rural Dean and finally becoming a Canon of Monmouth. He was very involved in the activities of the school and village and when he left in 1901 was presented with a "handsome gold watch". His wife received a "rich dress ring" and Mr Duck, on behalf of the bell ringers, gave him a set of tantalus.

Percy Mortimer, of whom locals still have fond memories, was born in Swansea in 1875, and was educated at Jesus College Oxford. He came to Penmark in 1901 after ten years at St Woolas, Newport. On his retirement twenty three years later, the parishioners marked their appreciation of his work by presenting to him and his wife:

> "a wallet of treasury notes, a silver rose bowl and a silver ink stand."

His wife was the first secretary of the Rhoose and Aberthaw nursing association and was presented with a handsome travelling case as a token of her valuable services. The jovial vicar used to cycle round his parish; he paid for the choir outing which was often to Southerndown and the bell ringers' annual supper at the Six Bells. The children of his day remember also the Sunday School outings when they went to Barry Island in waggons pulled by horses with shining harnesses bedecked with ribbons.

John David Evans was in his 50's when he arrived in the parish, having been vicar of many Rhondda churches. After 10 years he left to work in the Diocesan office in Llandaff. His place was taken by Rev. Price, who also was nearing the end of his ministry. Having had four vicars in forty years, the parish was then fortunate to get in

BURIALS in the Parish of Penmark in the County of Glamorgan in the Year 1895

Name.	Abode.	When buried.	Age.	By whom the Ceremony was performed.
Margaret Nash No. 777.	Penmark	January 12. 1895	2 months	Em Dr Hulst Roman Catholic Priest
Mary Rees No. 778.	Burton	7 February 1895	38 yrs	Edward Morgan Vicar
James Jones No. 779.	32 Castleland Street Barry	8 March 1895	72 yrs	A. J. Hughes Vicar of Llancarfan
David Eddols No. 780.	Burton	9 March 1895	70 yrs	Edward Morgan Vicar of Penmark
James Jones No. 781.	Fordogan	7 May 1895	80 yrs	Edward Morgan Vicar of Penmark
William Williams No. 782.	Parish of St. John Cardiff	13 August 1895	71 yrs	Edward Morgan Vicar of Penmark
Thomas Morgan No. 783.	Lamb'ethery	14 August 1895	29 yrs	Edward Morgan Vicar of Penmark
Thomas Henry Price No. 784.	Lambethery	14 August 1895	28 yrs	Edward Morgan Vicar of Penmark

7. *Church register burial 1895.*

1938 the services of William Hubert Williams, who stayed with them until his retirement thirty years later.

The church registers started in 1696, but the earliest now in existence is dated 1751. The entries in them record events (both happy and sad) in the lives of the parish inhabitants. Being a parish bordering the sea, there are many entries referring simply to "body on Beach", but one sea tragedy was well recorded.

> "On January 3rd 1880, were buried 5 Germans who perished in the wreck of the barque IDA of STRETTON which was cast on shore at Breaksea on the night of December 31st 1879. Four more of the same crew are buried at Porthkerry. One alone was saved".

The Western Mail reported the event and interviewed through an interpreter the only survivor. He stated:

> "The vessel left Cardiff with coal for Teneriffe, but when nearing Lundy Island the ever increasing fury of the storm compelled the captain to turn the vessel's head and endeavoured to return to Cardiff. It was dark and the sea was rolling high; water dashed on the deck with great violence and all at once the vessel struck, turned over and immediately split into fragments. I got along the main mast while the captain and others stayed with the wreckage. I was much knocked about by the water, but eventually gained the shore as I was nearer to it than the others through being at the end of the fallen mast. I could proceed no further having become insensible. Presently I awoke and seeing a light crawled on my hands and knees towards it and thus reached a house 300 yards distant having got over a wall."

He had arrived at Ocean House where a party was in progress (it was December 31st) and the guests rushed to the shore hoping to rescue the crew, but it was the following day before the bodies of the captain, mate, cook and six able seamen were recovered. The locals had never seen such a wreck and found it hard to believe that such a large vessel could have been broken up by the waves and thrown on the shore in such a confused heap. The only cargo to be seen were frequent lumps of coal, alternating with the pebbles along the coast.

A tragedy befalling a local family is recorded on January 23rd 1850.

> "Then were buried three Hughes children Mary aged 6, Eleanor aged 4 and Elizabeth aged 11 months. These three were buried in the same grave and in one coffin. They were burnt to death having been left alone at Watch House by their parents, the house having caught fire".

It is not unusual to find in the baptism registers reference to "base-born", "love-child", "father unknown" but the baptism of David John on 10th May 1827 is rather different. The vicar recorded

> "David son of James John labourer of Penmark, mother unknown."

Page 4

BAPTISMS solemnized in the Parish of Penmark in the County of Glamorgan in the Year 1895

When Baptised.	Child's Christian Name.	Parent's Name. Christian.	Surname.	Abode.	Quality, Trade, or Profession.	By whom the Ceremony was performed.
1895 March 6. 1895 born 26 Nov 1872 No. 25	Sarah Ann	William & Mary	Bennett	Penmark Vicarage	Forgeman	Edward Morgan Vicar
1895 Sep 11. 1895 born Aug 28 1895 No. 26	Albert James	John & Ann	Ball	Aberthaw	Labourer	Edward Morgan Vicar
1895 November 12. 1895 born 23 July 1891 No. 27	Ethel May	Thomas & Annie	Prior	Llancadle	Labourer	Edward Morgan Vicar
1895 November 12 1895 born 24 Sep 1895 No. 28	Ethel May	Charles & Catharine	Prior	Llancadle	Mason Labr	Edward Morgan Vicar
1895 November 16. 1895 No. 29	Margaret Sarah	David Walter & Mary Edith	Savours	Fonligary	Farmer	Edward Morgan Vicar
1896 February 16. 1896 born 1895 No. 30	Richard John	Henry Alfred & Lucy	Maden	Penmark	Police Constable	Edward Morgan Vicar
1896 February 16 1896 No. 31	Jane	William & Mary	Palmer	Penmark	Labourer	Edward Morgan Vicar
1896 April 12 born Feb 26th No. 32	Marjorie	Thomas & Rosa	Bowen	Penmark	Farmer	Edward Morgan Vicar

8. Church register baptism 1895.

On September 4th 1824 were baptised William, Owen and John, sons of Robert and Ann Mathews of Welford Farm. The vicar had noted in the register "these three at one birth". Another multiple birth in 1894 did not have such a happy ending, for the burial registers record:-

> Jane Nicholls was 5 minutes old when she died.
> Ann Nicholls was 30 minutes old when she died.

An early example of "name - dropping" can be found in the marriage register of 1759. The officiating minister signed his name and added, "Rector of Wenvoe and friend of John Wesley".

There are nearly 300 memorials in the well-kept churchyard which is still used for burials, in spite of the Council in 1931 saying they would no longer be responsible for the upkeep of the burial ground and a new one would soon be needed. The vicar was asked for his observations and he assured the Council that the present burial ground (churchyard) would always be carefully looked after by the church authorities, whether at any time it would be necessary for it to be closed or not.

A most imposing memorial is the large celtic cross behind the church in memory of the Jones family from Fonmon Castle. The funeral of Oliver Henry on January 9th 1917 was a large affair conducted by the incumbent and the Bishop of Llandaff. The body was carried from the Castle to the church by bearers consisting of estate tenants and members of the County constabulary. The local paper recorded that:

> "The whole of the County Police Force of Barry and District were present with a large contingent of Constabulary from other parts of the County."

NONCONFORMISTS and CATHOLICS

One thinks of the established church as the centre of village activities, with parishioners adhering to the rites of that church. This was not the case. The last century saw the emergence of non-conformity and many denominations were catered for, at first holding meetings in members' homes.

As mentioned, John Wesley preached from the Jacobean pulpit of St Mary's. Also, the Welsh revivalist Howell Harris visited the district in 1740 and inspired a Calvinistic Methodist cause which led to the opening of Sardis Chapel at Penmark in 1832. The building held over 200 people and was often full for the evening service, with over 100 people attending the morning one. At this time (1851) the St Mary's congregation was about 60 in the morning, including children and 30 in the evening. The Chapel Sunday School was also well attended and possibly the children were taught basic reading and writing. This was in the years before organised education was available and was of course free. The building was altered in 1880 and flourished until a new chapel was opened in Rhoose in 1931, built at a cost of £1,000. The deacon in 1851 was Thomas Mathews, a farmer from Fontygary; a later minister, Rev. Phillips, lived at the Manse at Llancadle. In 1892 the monthly meeting was held there for methodist ministers from the district. The local paper stated, "their conveyance to the village was by brakes

9. *Sefton Cottage c.1900 – named in Blackton Charity.*

10. *Jeremia and Mary Murphy outside Sefton Cottage.*

running from Cowbridge and Barry to meet the various trains. The utmost hospitality was shown by the inhabitants towards strangers". The minister for the previous five years was the Reverend Walter Daniel, who moved soon after this meeting to the expanding Barry Dock. The members presented him with a writing desk with his name engraved on it.

The Baptist movement was established in the Vale even earlier; Llancarfan had a chapel in 1823 and a branch of this was built at Aberthaw about 1870 served by the Rev. T.N. Sealey. In 1887 the Jubilee Hall was built in Rhoose by John Cory and used as a gospel mission, with Pastor Harding serving there for forty six years. It was sold to the Wesleyan methodists in 1938. There was also a mission hall opened at Aberthaw in 1897 which had an active Band of Hope group. The Welsh Independents built Salem chapel at Nurston in 1851.

For several years Penmark was the centre of the Catholic population in the region and known locally as "Little Ireland". The first Irish family to arrive in the Parish was James Tobin, with his wife and daughter in 1850. Within a decade ten per cent of the population of the parish was of Irish origin. Until 1862 they were served by priests who travelled from Cardiff and services were held in homes in the parish. The following account of the early years of Irish Catholicism in the Vale is taken from the Catholic magazine St Peter's Chair.

"The first of these priests was Father Nedelec (of the Fathers of Charity). Before coming, he sent a letter to get a place ready for him to give Benediction. That was found in the house of James Barry who worked for a farmer at Tredogan. When the farmer's wife found out the priest was coming she sent to stop him at once. The poor farmer being afraid of losing the house, went to meet Father Nedelec and told him his trouble, but the Rev Father told him never to mind, but go back with him and see what would happen. They had Benediction without any interruption. That being over it was settled that every one should pay sixpence a quarter to the Mission expenses. The next place the priest went to was Rhoose, to the house of William Neal, where they had Holy Mass. The next place was Fontygary in the house of Thomas Roberts. He said the squire would not be willing, but Father Nedelec drove up to the Castle and asked to see the Squire who admitted him, gave him lunch and freedom to preach the gospel in the surrounding district. Father Nedelec then went to Penmark, to the house of Jeremiah Daly".

After that came Father Bruno, who experienced great hardships. He celebrated Mass at Llanbethery for a number of years. One time, when the snow was a foot deep on the ground, he came from Cardiff to prepare an old woman for death. Part of the way he could come by train, but the rest he had to walk through the snow, the water oozing out of his boots. The subscription was raised to one shilling a quarter. He used to come out to instruct the children on weekdays, sometimes walking the whole distance there and back, twenty-four miles.

Father Bruno was succeeded by Father Hayde, who used to celebrate mass in the houses of Jeremiah Murphy, Daniel Holland, Owen McCarthy, Lawrence Driscoll and Denis Regan, at the Finger-Post in Penmark Village. He was followed by the Rev Father Clark who was in the area for about eight years, and celebrated Mass in the same houses. These services were continued on a more regular basis by Father Hyland, who was the first Catholic priest to officiate at St Mary's, when he buried Mary Daly in June 1880. Marriages still took place at St David's in Cardiff. By 1889 there were 146 Roman Catholics in the Parish and many were able to go to Mass in a small room at the thatched Wenvoe Arms at Cadoxton. An altar was erected each Sunday morning in a

Extracted from the Registry of the Consistory Court of Llandaff

In the last Will and Testament of William Jones late of Blackton in the parish of Penmark and County of Glamorgan gen deceased bearing date the twenty fourth day of December in the year of our Lord one thousand seven hundred and thirteen and now remaining in the said Registry is among other things the following devise. Viz

"First I do hereby give and devise and
"bequeath the yearly rents issues and profitts of
"two Acres and a halfe of freehold Lands
"together with a house and its appurtenants lately
"purchased by me Situate lying and being at
"Sufton in the said prish of Penmarke to the
"sole use and behoofe of the poor of the said
"prish of Penmarke for ever, And my Will
"and desire is that the Minister and Churchwardens
"and their Successors as Guardians and Trustees
"do and shall from year to year Annually lett
"the said house and two Acres and a half of
"Lands to the best advantage and upon every
"Thursday in passion Week yearly distribute
"according to the best of their Judgm.t All the rents
"issues and profitts of the said house and Lands
"amongst the poor of the said s.d prish for
"ever.

Proved at Landaff on the 20th day of January 1713/4 before the Chancellor &c on the Oath Margaret Vaughan the Sister of the deceased and sole Executrix in the Will named being first sworn well and faithfully to administer &c

Edw.d Stephens
Regr.

11. Will of William Jones of Blackton 1713.

room which served as the local court and furniture and sacristy were carried from Father Hyland's house in Lower Guthrie Street.

In May 1892 a school chapel was dedicated on Court Road by Bishop Hedley and the children at Penmark school attended the service. The Parish church of St Helens in Barry was dedicated in 1907. Mass continued to be celebrated at the Regan home (Holly Cottage) until a wooden hut (St Vincents) was dedicated in Rhoose in 1927 and Canon Quigly celebrated the first mass.

CHARITIES

A report by the Commissioners for Charities in England and Wales 30th June 1837 refers to several charities, all of which were still operative at the time of a public meeting of the Charities Commission held in the National School in April 1895. The most substantial was called Jones's Charity. William Jones, of Blackton in the parish, by a Will, dated 24th December 1713, allocated the yearly rents and profits of 2 Acres 2 Roods of freehold land and a house, situate at Sefton, to the sole use of the poor of the parish of Penmark, for ever. The Will directed that the minister and churchwardens, as trustees, should let the said premises, and distribute the rents among the poor, according to the best of their judgement, on Thursday in Passion-week yearly. In 1837, the property consisted of a cottage in good repair, situated within 100 yards South-East of the road leading from Penmark to Fonmon; it was subdivided into two dwellings, each of which had a garden. They were let at rents amounting to £3, from which was deducted about 10s. for repairs. At the back of the gardens was an enclosure containing two acres and a half, which was let at a yearly rent of £4, subject to 2s. for land-tax. One of these cottages was occupied by Jeremiah Murphy and his family for many years. The rents were regularly paid on Good Friday, and distributed on the same day (together with the interest arising under the following gifts of various donors, and of a donor, unknown) by the vicar, churchwardens, and overseers, to poor parishioners not receiving parish relief, a preference being given to widows. The list of recipients was gone through publicly, and any fresh applications were considered. Every labourer in the parish benefited according to his requirements. The accounts books list the recipients and the amount received; about 40 people benefited each year with amounts varying from 2/6 to 7/-.

Among the donors referred to above were an unknown donor, who at a period unknown, but before 1786, gave £20: the Rev. Rowland Jay, who in 1779, gave £12/10s and William Alexander, who in 1797, gave £10 to the use of the poor not receiving parochial relief. These sums, having, in 1807, come into possession of the parishioners, were by them lent to the Rev. J.T. Casberd D.C.L, for the repayment of which, with interest at 5 per cent, he gave his note of hand. The sum of £42-10s. mentioned in the report of 1837 was in the year 1843 given into the safekeeping of R.O. Jones Esq. of Fonmon Castle, who regularly paid the interest, at the rate of 5 per cent, during his lifetime and Mr H.O. Jones, his son, did so after him. In 1895, Mr. Jones proposed to pay the principal to the trustees of the Charity. The suggestion of transferring the money to the Official Trustees of Charitable Funds was not favourably received, on the ground that the interest derived from Consols (presumably meaning Government consolidated

Money distributed on Good Friday Mar. 25. 1864

James Evan's not[e]	1 – 10 – 0	
Jane Deere do	1 – 10 – 0	
Money in Savings bank	12 – 0	
Mr Thomas' not[e]	4 – 0 – 0	
R. O. Jones Esq[r]. interest	2 – 2 – 6	
	£9 – 14 – 6	

Name	s	d	Name	s	d
S. Hopkin	4		W[m] Evan	10	
W Williams (Furnace)	5		Tho[s]. William (Blacklay)	5	
Jo[s] Evan	3	6	John Jones	4	6
Tho[s]. Thomas (Pennaske)	6		Edw[d] Wilson	4	
Jo[s] Smith	4		Timothy Kemp	2	6
Jo[s] Thomas Penylan	5		John Rees (Park)	2	6
Tho[s]. Jenkin	5		Dav[d]. Griffiths	2	6
David Lewis	3		W Morgan	4	
John Rees (Furnace)	7		John Eddolls	4	
Tho[s]. Edwards	3		Jerry Daly	3	
Edward Rees	6		Rich[d] Deere	2	6
Edw[d] Williams	4		W[m] Evan	2	6
Tho[s] James Sen[r]	6	6	John Bryan	2	6
John Thomas	6		Tho[s]. James Barber	2	6
John Hopkin	4		Jo[s]. Barry	2	6
Morgan Deere	6		John Power	2	
Tho[s]. Lewis	4		H. Toby	2	
W. Rees Furnace	5		In hand		
W Hopkin	5		M. Evans		
W Morgan Whitland	4				
Henry David	4				
John Sullivan	3				
Jos. Toby	3		Rates &c	5	
John Miles	3				
Edw[d] James	5			9	14
Florry Mahoney	3				
David Thomas	4				
Mike Murray	4				
Dennis Bohege	3				
Rich[d] Magey	4				
	6 11 0				

12.   *Charity distribution 1864.*

stocks used for investments by the Official Trustees of Charitable Funds) would be only half the present rate. The £20 from the unknown donor had been secured on a mortgage. This having been paid off, on the 24th March 1830 it was deposited in the Cardiff savings' bank, in the names of the vicar, churchwardens, and officers, and 13s, the interest, was regularly paid in March or April. In 1862, monies for distribution amounted to £9-14-6. The capital of this Charity was deposited in the Post Office Savings Bank at Cowbridge. The bank pass book showed a balance on 31st December 1894 of £22-1s-9d, the increase being caused by accumulation of interest kept in hand by the trustees for expenses connected with the buildings belonging to Jones's Charity. The yearly interest was 10s.

Charity receipts and distribution

April 1875

Income		Expenses	
R.O. Jones (interest)	2- 2-6	Due to Mr Alexander	6-5
Savings Bank	12-0	Mr Shelmake (thatcher)	1-10-0
T Thomas (rent)	4- 0-0	T. Lewis for spars	7-6
James Evans (rent)	1-10-0	Distributed amongst poor	7- 1-6
James Lewis (rent)	1-10-0	Balance	9-4
	9-14-6		9-14-6

39 people received monies ranging from 7/- to 2/-

1895

Balance	4-11	
O.H. Jones	2- 2-06	
A. Thomas (rent)	4-10-00	
Jeremiah Murphy	3- 00-00	
John Murphy	3- 00-00	
	12- 5-05	£10-4-0- distributed
1900 Distributed	£8-4-6	to 50 people
1920 "	£6-15-0	to 40 people
1924 "	£7- 4-6	to 40 people

Income and distribution continued at the same rates until the war, even though some people were only receiving 2/6. At a District Council meeting in 1938 the Sefton cottages were said to be "unfit for human habitation and not capable at reasonable expense of being rendered so fit". They had to be vacated within twenty-eight days and demolished within six weeks. This directive must have been ignored as the rent continued to be paid for four more years. The cottages eventually burnt down, but the land was still available to rent in accordance with the conditions of the charity.

When a person could no longer work through age or infirmity they had to turn to the Parish or the workhouse for relief. Few local people during the period I have covered ended their days in the workhouse, but quite a few received "outdoor relief" of up to 4s. per week from the Cardiff Union for many years and were able to stay in their own homes. Unfortunately the wording of the Blackton charity prevented these needy people from receiving extra relief.

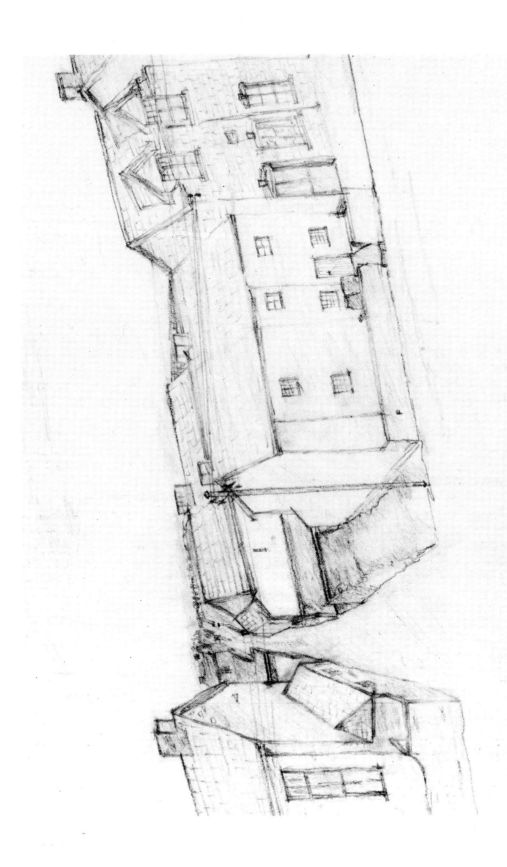

School Circa 1940 Post Office

THE VESTRY

Prior to Parish and District Councils, local administration was carried out by the Vestry. Although originally a church committee, it usually consisted of prominent parishioners of all denominations. One of its functions was to levy a Parish rate; it also appointed Overseers of the poor, kept law and order and maintained local footpaths. It was the job of the Overseer of the Poor to give relief to parishioners in need, either in money or in kind. This was a voluntary, but unpopular office and was not abolished until 1925.

In 1861, the vestry allowed Mr Evans, the Assistant Overseer, £1 for his expenses in reference to an order made for the removal of certain paupers from the parish and in March, the following year, he was paid £2-13-9 for the removal of Joanna Yorath. He resigned in 1864 and two years later the minutes record that Mrs Evans was allowed £2-9-5 in consideration of the late Mr Evans' services.

In 1859 £10 was given by the parish towards the repair of Merthyr Dyfan Rd., provided that the improvement be maintained by the Highways Board. A similar sum was allowed towards widening the road near to Penmark Vicarage and making a fence adjoining glebe land. The village well was repaired in 1873 and in 1883 a copy of the first edition Ordnance Survey map was bought so that rights of way could be recorded. In 1900 Mrs Smith, the caretaker, had her salary increased to £6-10-0 and she and her assistant were both insured against accident whilst employed in the churchyard. Sundry payments were made between 1907 and 1913 for gravel for the churchyard footpath, cleaning inside the church, clearing the churchyard and new curtains for the vestry. Extra lamps were also provided for better lighting of the church.

In 1897 John Alexander retired as churchwarden after at least twenty years service. His place was taken by Mr T. Harbottle, who together with Mr O.H. Jones as vicar's warden, stayed in office until 1917. Mrs O.H. Jones became vicar's warden on the death of her husband.

In March 1913 and April 1914 a proposal was made that the Vestry meeting of the parish of Penmark protest against the Bill for the Disestablishment and Disendowment of the Church in Wales and pledge itself to do all in its powers to prevent the bill becoming law. The following year the Vestry urged Parliament to pass the Welsh Act Postponement Bill without delay and thus relieve the anxiety of church people in the present crisis. Their efforts were in vain, for although the war delayed immediate action, the Anglican Church in Wales was disestablished in 1920.

PARISH COUNCIL

The local Government Act of 1894 transferred responsibilities for local administration to the Parish Council, but the Vestry continued to administer the affairs of the church. Initially people were elected to the Council for a year, but after the 1901 election, Councillors would remain in office for three years. At first a quorum was three Councillors, but subsequently this was reduced to two when three consecutive meetings had to be cancelled for want of a quorum.

Penmark Parish Council had its first meeting in January 1895. Its members were people who were prominent in village or parish activities. They were Matthew Evans,

14. *Penmark Main Street c1935 showing Six Bells.*

Thomas Harbottle, O.H. Jones, William James, Thomas Jones, Rev. Morgan and William Reese. O.H. Jones was the first chairman and remained in office until his death in 1917. T. Harbottle became clerk and he and W. James were appointed overseers of the poor, positions they held for twelve years.

An agenda was set at the first meeting for obtaining allotments and improving the state of the cottages, many of which were in a dilapidated state. Later, the Council became involved in the provisions for refuse disposal, upkeep of footpaths and stiles, provision of bus services, water supplies and electricity. The period from 1894 to 1950 saw many changes in the provision of services for the parish and the Council was involved in these things either directly or by calling on the services of the District or County Councils. There were many opportunities for delays because there was some lack of clarity in the borderline between the duties and responsibilities of the Parish Council and the District Council.

Not surprisingly, there were also some local boundary disputes. In 1931 an acrimonious meeting took place between Porthkerry and Penmark Councils. The former wanted to extend their boundary to include "that portion from Fontygary to Fonmon Cross and from there to Rhoose Cross." Penmark rejected this idea. The District Council suggested the two parishes combine at which stage Penmark refused any further discussion and requested the whole matter be dropped. The County Council was still in favour of combining the two parishes, so Penmark Council called a parish meeting on Dec 31 1931 to "protest strongly against the amalgamation of Porthkerry and Penmark parishes being convinced that no good result or economy can be obtained by such an amalgamation". This protest would be sent to the County Council, District Council and if necessary the Minister of Health!

The first clerk to the Council was paid £5 a year, this increased in 1931 to £15. In 1933, it was suggested that the payment be increased to £30 as it was lower than any other in the area. However, it was considered inadvisable due to the depression in trade and was only increased to £20. When Mr Roberts resigned in 1936, after twelve years in office, 13 people applied for the job. It was decided that it should be given to a local ex-serviceman and this reduced the applicants to Mr G. Watkins and Mr Morris. Both were interviewed and Mr Watkins was appointed, but resigned on health grounds after only two years. He was succeeded by Mr Bassett, who held the position until 1955.

In 1936 it was realised that Mrs Duck still had in her house the safe bought in 1906 for £6-6s, plus 2s. carriage, when her husband was clerk. Mr Roberts was directed to inspect it and, if in good condition, move it to his home. The cost for transporting it was 7s.!

ALLOTMENTS

In January 1894 eight people applied for allotments. They were M. Murray, who wanted 1 acre of arable land for a garden, W. Thomas (1 acre for pasture), J.Dunscombe (3 acres for pasture and 1 acre for arable), D. Bryan, J. Mahoney, W. Vizard, T. Roberts and Jerry Murphy all applied for 1/4 acres for garden purposes. The allotment committee set about finding four acres of land to rent for this purpose. There was no immediate success, but they persevered during 1895. At that time Mr Shirley (a land agent) was prepared to release 4 acres for rent at a price of £4 per acre, which compared

15. *Penmark Post Office c.1925 possibly Mr. & Mrs. Thomas.*

with 20 to 30 shillings per acre for rent of land for farming. Those wanting allotments were not prepared to pay more than £2 per acre. In view of this difference, the County Council was asked whether it would be prepared to give the Parish Council power to hire land compulsorily in accordance with the local government Act of 1894. By this time (August 1895) the number of applicants had dwindled to six people; Mr Dunscombe was not prepared to take arable without pasture and J. Murphy withdrew. The six were prepared to accept 1/4 acre each, but two years later the Parish Council was informed that the demand was too small to justify action by the County Council and that they should look for a small piece of arable land. There the matter rested until 1908 when a public meeting was called to hear O.H. Jones explain the provisions of the Allotment and Small Holdings Act and to receive applications for allotments. Only two people applied, and one acre of land was applied for in Fonmon. The Council minutes do not record if it was ever allocated.

HOUSING AND SANITATION

In 1894 several cottages were identified as in need of repair and some were said to have an inadequate supply of "offices" ie closets or toilets. The Parish Council asked the owners to repair them and to provide more office accommodation. The Inspector of Nuisances regularly visited the parish and the following are taken from his reports.

> 3 houses in the Cwm with damp walls and damp and broken floors.
> Jane Rees - cottage near post office with foul closet.
> Sefton Cottage - foul closet and piggeries.
> Barren Hill cottage in filthy condition.
> James Smith - pigsty want of efficient drainage and paving.

When a notice had been served on the owner or landlord, they had to rectify the nuisance as soon as possible. If they failed to do so the surveyor would authorise the work and reclaim the costs. In 1905, Mrs Goodway, at a house near to the post office, was reported for throwing slopwater onto the highway and the Council were ordered to remove "the accumulation of household rubbish near the Post Office".

In 1914 the Clerk was asked to write to the District Council asking them to arrange for a scavenger's cart to go through Aberthaw once or twice a week. A notice board would be placed near the refuse heap above Cuckoo Mill prohibiting the throwing of slop water. William Thomas put in a tender for 30s. to supply a notice board, but this was rejected and the chairman of the District Council was authorised by his committee to supply one at a lower cost. In view of the unsanitary state of the refuse tip in Penmark, it was decided in December 1928 to ask the District Council to provide a bin or covered-in receptacle instead of an open pit. The inspector suggested it be done away with and the sanitary cart would call at the village once a week. Two years later rubbish was still being thrown into the pit so a sign was erected prohibiting this. It was requested that the cart come earlier in the day. A complaint was also made to the sanitary inspector regarding the poor cleaning of the refuse tip. The scavengers cart was still going through the village during the War, and Henry Nation was paid £45 per annum for this task.

16. *Pleasant Harbour.*

FOOTPATHS AND HIGHWAYS

From the early days of the Council, there was constant activity to keep the footpaths and highways in acceptable condition. On one occasion the clerk wrote to the Surveyor of highways asking him to give instructions for the repair of the wall which had fallen down on the road leading from Penmark Village to the pump and to draw his attention to the road from the back of the vicarage to Fonmon Road, especially noting the dangerous condition of that part near the pump where the river runs at a much lower level than the road without the slightest protection of a boundary wall. He was asked to suggest the advisability of having the large stones in the road raised and broken. After a meeting with the surveyor, a response six months later reported that it should be rolled as much as possible and gravel be put down.

In 1898 Mr Alexander had applied for repairs to his stile. The Parish Council told him that "a stile is a fence and is not the responsibility of the Parish Council".

A new road was proposed in 1898 by the District Council to avoid the dangerous hill from the village towards Llancarfan. This was Barren Hill where people had been living for many years and which was used to get to the well and the Rose and Crown at Kenson. Local Councillors were invited to meet the District surveyor to discuss the best direction for the road. At the same time the Parish Council took the initiative to ask for a wall to be built between the road and the field adjoining the vicarage near to the gate and in response a fence was erected. Instructions were given to place a new stile near the road, to clear the footpath leading through Mr Thomas' garden to the corner of Mr Williams' field, to repair stiles and footpaths through the wood near Kenson Brook and to fence the whole length of the ditch near Penmark pump.

In 1919 the estimate for repairing the footpath through Penmark Place fields was £45. This was said to be too much, unless it included haulage of 60 loads of ashes. Kenson Bridge was reported to be in a bad state of repair and the village roads needed tar spraying.

At the end of 1921 the footpath through Penmark Wood and the Croft was repaired at a cost of £1 10s, but overhanging branches of trees and tree stumps on Barren Hill were still a nuisance.

In 1923 tenders were sought for repairing three stiles in footpaths between Penmark and Windmill Rd. Local tradesmen tendered as follows- Mr Williams £7-10; Mr James £6-6s; Mr Roberts £7; Mr Thomas £4-18-6. The cheapest tender secured the work.

A letter was sent to the tenant at Croft John drawing his attention to the condition of the public footpath between the stiles owing to the trespass of a horse. In 1927 an estimate for a stone stile with three pipes at the foot of vicarage hill was deemed expensive and the Council finally settled for a cheaper concrete one by Mr James at £3-18-6. Mr Williams replaced the footpath across four brooks from Penmark to Welford for £3.00.

The approach to the footbridge at Cuckoo Mill was dangerous, there being no protection for the path so that anyone attempting to cross in darkness could easily mistake the footpath and would walk into the river. Rails were needed on both sides.

In 1925, Messrs James (£5-7-6) and Thomas (£5-17-6) tendered for a stile at Higher End and a footpath to Llancarfan, but the footbridge at the bottom of Penmark Hill had to be repaired at once and Mr Vizard did this at £1-5-0. Mr James was paid £4 to erect concrete posts and tubular rails to the footbridge over the brook at the foot of vicarage hill.

WESTERN MAIL & SOUTH WALES NEWS, WEDNESDAY, FEBRU

"TIRADE" PROTEST | ROAD

AT THE VILLAGE PUMP in Penmark.

VILLAGERS RATIONED FOR WATER

Bucketful a Day From Council's Cart

By OUR SPECIAL CORRESPONDENT

Within ten miles of Cardiff, a city with one of the finest water supplies in the land, there are villages where the inhabitants draw a precarious ration of water from the local pump, just as did their forebears generations back.

I have specially in mind the villages of Penmark, Fonmon, and Aberthaw in the beautiful Vale of Glamorgan. If you stroll thereabouts you will see the men, women, and children carrying water to their homes in buckets during any weather, but when it is fine they do not hurry overmuch, for the well was always everywhere a meeting place for local gossip.

Idyllic though this may appear to be there is little poetry in the talk of the Penmark folk when they discuss the

AT THE SIGN OF THE BLUE BELL

"Come Back and Sin No More" Gospel

By TOM MACDONALD

I have been to a meeting of an unusual society of women, The True Friend in Need Society, at the house of Mrs. Margaret Morgan, known by the sign of the Blue Bell, Mill-street, in the parish of Aberdare, in the county of Glamorgan.

Once every four weeks they meet at the sign of the Blue Bell. They each pay 6d. at every meeting, and all the money goes into a box.

What a box! It has three locks and three keys, one for each of the stewards (stewardesses, really) and the other for the landlady of the house, Mrs. Margaret Morgan.

A couple who were absent from the

In 1936 there was grave danger of flooding on Barren Hill because the culvert was full of stones and a proper water course was requested.

Wooden railings at the bottom of "sudden death hill", Penmark, near the vicarage had collapsed and the County Council was asked to replace them with something of a more permanent nature such as concrete posts and pipe railings. The County Council replied that as the parish had erected the fence, it was their responsibility. The chairman Sir Seymour Boothby said that as this hill borders the public highway, the highways authority was responsible and they eventually erected a fence "of a permanent nature".

WATER

Until this century, village people relied on natural sources for their water supply. In Penmark there were three wells; a large one near the Cwm fed from the stream and smaller ones at Sefton and Kenson. A favourite way of carrying water from the well was by means of a yoke which was a wooden frame cut and shaped to fit around the neck and over the shoulders. Two buckets were suspended from this by chains. Water carts - high barrels on wheels pulled by horses were used for larger quantities with the horses going right into the stream.

In July 1898, Mr Dunscombe reported that water in his well at Kenson was unfit for drinking purposes. He was advised to see the agent Mr Frazer and if he refused to act, the clerk would write to him. The following year it was suggested to the surveyor that a pump be placed on Sefton Well similar to that at Nurston and this was done.

The first attempt to pipe water to the Parish was in December 1899 when a Parish meeting was called to consider the advisability of extending the water supply from Rhoose to Penmark. A large attendance heard Mr Frazer, the Engineer and Surveyor to the District Council, explain the course and cost. The plan was to run the pipes from Rhoose to Fontygary, East Aberthaw, Burton, Fonmon and Penmark. This was 8820 yards. After much discussion the Vicar proposed and Mr O.H. Jones seconded that "having considered the scheme and cost, the Parish does not see its way to adopt the scheme at the present time". This was carried unanimously.

An estimate in 1926 for repair to Kenson well was £20. An alternative scheme was to lay a one inch pipe from Penmark well to the roadside near Barren Hill cottages, providing there was sufficient fall. Penmark well was to have a new door and lock and to be cleaned. A new trough had been put on the pump in 1907 when it was decided to keep the door locked and give the clerk custody of the key.

In 1931 The District Council was asked for a scheme by which water could be brought from Penmark Well to the village. The answer was that this was not possible and a quote was requested for laying water mains from Welford Farm to Aberthaw along Port Road so that Fonmon and Penmark could also be supplied.

In 1932 the Council unanimously suggested that the water scheme be carried out and if the parish meeting disagree, then Aberthaw and Penmark should be connected. The 14 members at the meeting in May were against connection as a whole, but an amendment was passed agreeing to connection for Penmark and Aberthaw.

The Western Mail early in 1934 had photographs of villagers drawing "a precarious ration of water" from the well. It went on to report that children on returning from school

18. *Penmark Pump c.1928.*

"have to scramble down the hill with buckets and climb back heavy laden before they can have a cup of tea. Washing day is heart-breaking, for every drop of water has to be brought up the steep hill. As for baths, they are a luxury which can be obtained only rarely".

Later that year an Inquiry was held in connection with the loan required for the proposed water scheme and the Council approached the District Council regarding employment of local labour when work started. In April 1935 J. Harry and Son of Radyr successfully tendered £5896-19-2d for the scheme to extend the mains to Penmark, Aberthaw and Fonmon. (There were nine tenders, the highest being for £10626-1-0d). In October 1935, Mr Bassett asked the Parish Council for street lighting but was urged to "refrain from pressing the matter until the present water scheme had been completed". When the work was finally completed over thirty years after it was first suggested, the village pumps were still retained as in most cases, there was only one cold water tap per cottage.

LIGHTING AND ELECTRICITY

Efforts to get electricity into the parish took even longer than the water saga. A special meeting was called in November 1896 to consider the advisability of adopting the Lighting and Watching Act of 1833, but the idea was rejected.

In 1907 the Council agreed to buy two lamps for use at the Parish Council meetings in the schoolroom. The cost was £2-10s each plus 1/7 carriage and 4/- for fitting.

Six electors in November 1936 asked for a Parish meeting to discuss electric lights for the Fontygary road area. The Council discussed this request and suggested that the villages of Penmark, Aberthaw and Fonmon might also benefit from such a scheme. Villagers were canvassed for their views; they were in favour providing there would not be an extortionate increase in the parish rate. A meeting was held at Berkeley Cafe, Rhoose with Mr James as chairman. Mr Pyne the District Councillor outlined the scheme and costs. After much discussion it was resolved that "this meeting be adjourned as the time is not opportune to adopt the street lighting act and stands deferred".

Further delays occurred until it was known if all the parish would have to pay if only part of it was lit. Various discussions followed, but in May 1937 the District Council approved a scheme to supply electricity to Llancarfan, Bonvilston, Fonmon and Penmark as the parishioners were prepared to pay, for the time being, 6d per unit in order to obtain a supply. They also applied to the Electricity Commissioners to borrow £5,000 in respect of the cost of the scheme which was extended a few months later to include Tredogan at an additional cost of £270. Negotiations then took place to agree the position of poles to carry the overhead wires and many difficulties were encountered with wayleaves. In April 1938, Mr Noon at Gileston House complained that the erection of a pole in the footpath outside his house had undermined the foundation of his boundary wall and would be a danger to his property in high winds. The District engineer wrote to reassure him that "there was no reason to anticipate that the wall and pole would fall down in windy weather"; in fact both are still standing today. To get a supply to the vicarage, the vicar had to guarantee to consume electricity to the value of

19. *Penmark Pump 1935.*

£10 for five years. Mr Radcliffe at Penmark Place agreed a minimum payment of £6 per annum for the extension of the mains to the farm. A parish meeting in July gave the Council power to raise £150 loan for capital charges and maintenance for the first year and to proceed as soon as possible, but there were now delays in the delivery of materials owing to the War Crisis.

Early in 1939 the street lights were erected as follows:- 27 lamps of 75 watts with mounting brackets, 3 to be placed at Aberthaw, 7 at Penmark, 2 at Fonmon Road, 4 at Fonmon and 11 at Rhoose. The cost for fixing was £3 per lamp and the maintenance charges were £2-4-0 per lamp if lit from sunset to midnight with an extra 1/- per quarter if the lamps were on for the two winter quarters. The first payment for street lighting was £32 6 0 on June 30th 1939. Having waited so long, there was a certain irony in the fact that the lights could not be used because of the black-out.

Electricity offered a new way of cooking and demonstrations were given in the area from the "specially fitted Demonstration coach of the Jackson Electric Company Ltd". Over 100 people attended these demonstrations and it was anticipated that about twenty people would apply for a cooker. These were not usually bought, but hired.

SOCIAL EVENTS

In the early part of the 19th century, holidays as we know them today were unknown. Work for many was 7 days a week, 52 weeks of the year; the exception being Christmas day and possibly Good Friday. For this reason any National or local event meriting a holiday was greeted with enthusiasm. Until the mid 19th century, Penmark parish held its annual three day wake or revel in August and there was a fair held in the village in the "little fields" every year. It was a noisy exciting day with steam engines of all shapes and sizes, livestock sales, and hawkers and peddlers selling their wares. The Irish community were always in good voice, O'Donnell's Wake being a favourite song.

> There was Dicky Price and Foster
> And old Jack Jones the coster
> Batty Jones and Steve O'Donague,
> There were writers, there were blighters
> There were were men of high position
> There were Irish politicians
> And they all got drunk at Steve O'Donnell's wake.

By the beginning of the 20th century, the fair was reduced to stalls on the roadside below the church. Another event meriting a school holiday was the ploughing match held on Windmill Lane. This was started in October 1896 and was open to all comers in Glamorgan and Monmouth who had not won a major prize in a similar event. The day finished with a dinner at the Six Bells hosted by the publican.

Holidays were celebrated by the school on other special occasions and were recorded in the Headmaster's log book. This records a day's holiday on March 10 1863 to celebrate the wedding of the Prince of Wales; a half day holiday on August 5th 1870 when the vicar gave a Treat to the children and took them to the seaside; a whole day

20.   *Rose and Crown c.1900.*

holiday in January 1874 in consequence of the marriage of Miss Jones and two years later another day's holiday for the wedding of the vicar's daughter. In 1879 there was a half day holiday for a tea party held at the chapel and in July 1889 there was a day's holiday outing to the opening of the new Barry Dock. The Diamond Jubilee of Queen Victoria in 1897 must have been especially welcome to the community because it was commemorated in June by a week's holiday and, on the 20th the parishes of Penmark and Porthkerry combined in a day's sports and celebration in a spacious field at Penmark. The ladies from the two parishes worked assiduously to provide tea in the school after which sixty four children were presented with mugs. In the evening there was a firework display. The whole was arranged by Rev. Morgan with the assistance of Messrs Duck, James Lougher, W Allen, J Saviours, W Thomas, T Bowen and T Jones who acted as stewards, judges and starters. The balance in hand from the jubilee fund was used to place a bell on the school. This was rung daily to call the children to school until it eventually cracked after about twenty year's use and was removed. In May 1898, the relief of Mafeking was celebrated with a tea party for parents and children with sports and games. Afterwards, they heard the vicar deliver a short address on the war and had cheers for Lord Roberts and Baden Powell. The day ended with the singing of the National Anthem.

There was tea and sports at Fonmon Castle on the occasion of the marriage of O.H. Jones in 1900. In 1902 the Boer war ended and there was a day's holiday in honour of the Declaration of Peace between Great Britain and South Africa. The celebrations for National events were usually organised by the Parish Council with the involvement of the vicar and headmaster. A public meeting called to consider the best way of commemorating the Coronation of King Edward VII heard their Chairman propose demonstrations similar to those held at the Diamond Jubilee of the late Queen Victoria and promised a donation of £3 from himself and £1 on behalf of Mrs Jones.

Although the local government board gave the Parish Councils authority to levy a rate to defray any costs it was agreed no rate be made in the parish, but all expenses be defrayed by voluntary subscription. Similarly, in 1910 fifteen people were present at the meeting called to consider the best way of commemorating the Coronation of King George V. The vicar was in the chair and Mr Duck acted as treasurer and secretary. Subsequently there was disappointment when it was announced that a week's holiday planned for the Coronation was postponed indefinitely as His Majesty had undergone an operation. However, the event was celebrated in 1911 in a field near Fonmon Castle lent by T. Harbottle. Again it was tea and sports, but the day started at 10:30am when a peal of the church bells announced the opening of the day's rejoicing. A special service followed at eleven o'clock. All the children under 14 were presented with a Coronation mug and a bag of sweets when they went home at 9:00pm.

Prizes were presented by Mrs. O.H. Jones in the absence of her husband who had been commanded by His Majesty to attend the coronation service in Westminster Abbey.

The Silver Jubilee Committee in 1935 under the chairmanship of Mr Boothby invited Porthkerry to send five members and make it a combined celebration. They refused this request to join an occasion which was "a wonderful success, thanks to the untiring efforts of the committee".

A public meeting was called in October 1936 to discuss the proposed memorial to George V and the Coronation of Edward VIII. Public collections were organised for the

21. *The Hunt c.1938.*

memorial fund which resulted in £12-10-3d being collected. In spite of previous problems a joint meeting with Porthkerry was proposed for the Coronation celebrations with expenses to be on a 50-50 basis. The Coronation celebrations would be held on May 12 with children over 3 catered for and sports for all in an open field similar to the Jubilee celebrations. A concert would be held at a later date. £35 was spent on the activities, which compared with £50 for VE celebrations in 1945. The County Council offered to provide five trees as a suitable memorial to George V. The Parish Council decided in May that these would be planted as follows - the old garage pump in Rhoose, in front of the church gate at Penmark, on an island in the centre of the pond at Fonmon, on spare ground at Tredogan and near the station approach at Aberthaw. It was later realised that road widening at Rhoose and Aberthaw meant the position of trees there would have to be reconsidered and as no one knew who owned the island in the pond, that idea would have to be abandoned also. In December the District Council decided that only one tree was to be allowed and that would be planted in the north east corner of the plantation in front of the school in Rhoose if the education committee agreed. This copper beech tree was planted by Lady Boothby on February 3rd 1938.

The Parish Council suggested placing a seat at Tredogan to commemorate the coronation.

WAR ACTIVITIES

Penmark was not untouched by "war effort". Apart from delays in completing the electricity scheme, there were some activities of note. For example, on September 22nd 1915, South Glamorgan war emergency committee asked the Parish Council to form a committee to carry on the work in the Parish. In January 1918 a letter from the War Agricultural committee specified the variety of potatoes allowed to be grown in Glamorgan and orders were received for 9 tons 4 cwt. Hay and horses were commandeered for the war without notice by the army authorities.

The first World War altered the community way of life. Five parishioners who lost their lives are listed on the war memorial inside the church. Local men served with the South Wales Borderers; Royal Engineers; Infantry and Royal Artillery. The news of the ending of this war was first received at the Castle which had the only phone in the Village.

An extraordinary general meeting was held in September 1938 to deal with the question of "air raid precautions due to the crisis". There was an urgent need for gas masks and it was imperative that the number of adults and children in the parish was recorded. The masks had not been delivered by the middle of 1939. The A.R.P officer for the Parish was Mr Evans who may have been the "suitable person nominated for the purpose of extinguishing the electric lamps in an emergency". There was a central control point in each parish for this purpose. The Village had its own air raid shelter, the cellar at the Croft, which was no doubt used on the night of April 29th 1941 when there were widespread raids on South Wales. This may have been the occasion when scatter bombs were dropped shattering windows in the church and Six Bells and causing damage to the ceiling at Penmark Farm.

22. *Fonmon School c.1890.*

THE SCHOOL

According to the Charity Commissioners' report of 1895, prior to 1846 the building now known as Penmark Village Centre was owned by the parish. In August 1846 it was sold to the Church for £30. The sale is recorded in an indenture dated 1st August 1846, and made between the Guardians of the Poor of the Cardiff Union, the overseers of the poor of the parish of Penmark and the churchwardens of the one part, and the Lord Bishop of Llandaff, the Archdeacon of Llandaff and the Rev. Charles Frederick Bryan Wood (vicar of the parish of Penmark) of the other part. The indenture records that

> "in consideration of the sum of £30 a property in the village of Penmark containing in length 48 feet, and in width 24 feet or thereabout, belonging to the said parish of Penmark and lately used for the reception of the poor is transferred to the church to be used solely as a site for a Sunday School and day school for poor persons in the parish of Penmark and for the residence of the master, mistress, teacher or teachers of the said schools and for no other purpose, the said school to be for ever thereafter in union with the National Society for promoting the education of the poor in the principles of the Established Church".

The indenture specified that the school would be managed by a committee, that the minister for the time being of the parish should have the superintendence of the religious instruction of the scholars and that any difference between the minister and the committee should be determined by the Bishop of the diocese. In all other respects the management of the school should vest in and be exercised by a committee consisting of the minister and three other persons. The first three appointed were Robert Oliver Jones, Esq, the Rev William Rayer, and Edward Romilly, Esq, all members of the Church of England and residents or entitled to at least a part of real property situated in the parish, and subscribers in the current year to the amount of 20 shillings at least to the school. Any vacancy had to be filled by a person or persons having a like qualification, "accepted by the subscribers to the school to the amount of 10 shillings per annum at the least and qualified in other respects as the persons to be elected". The Committee had power to appoint a committee of not more than four people being members of the Church of England, to assist in the visitation and engagement of the girls and infant scholars.

The present building, as the deed mentions, was used as a poor house, and owned by the parish until its sale in 1846. Part of the building was used as a school before that date. Mr Alexander stated that he attended the school in 1820. It is thought that the building had been used in the past for the Courts Leet. In 1847 it was described as "the old church-house". At that time, the building had upper and lower rooms and an external stone staircase. A Sunday school and a day school were held in the upper room. The ground floor had been used as alms houses but was then used as the vestry room and the schoolmaster's house. It stayed like this until 1895 when the building was altered and modernised and opened as the Penmark National School, which it remained until 1933, when the children were transferred to a new school at Rhoose.

From the early part of the the nineteenth century there was a private school at Fonmon for boys and girls, lying at the side of the park and surrounded by garden. After

23. *Penmark School Pupils 1897.*

Penmark village school was established, this became girls only. A report in 1847 stated that one boy was at the school, but he was lame and so was unable to walk to Penmark. It also states:

> "the school is comfortable and pretty and kept very neat and clean. The walls are well supplied with prints of natural history. The mistress conducts the school well, her manner is very good and the children are orderly".

The building, was originally thatched, and I believe continued as a school almost to the end of the century. It was then made into two dwellings to be used as homes for Castle employees.

The Penmark village school log book from 1863 records daily events at the school and also His Majesty's Inspector of Schools annual reports. These reports regularly indicated that until the arrival of Mr Duck, the standard was below average, possibly because no teacher stayed more than two years. Teachers were paid according to the percentage attendance of the pupils, and the grant allocated to the school depended on the standards achieved. Free schooling was not available until 1891 and the children in the early days paid between one and three old pennies (1d and 3d) on Mondays. Although legislation in 1876 stated that all children should receive elementary education, attendance did not become compulsory until 1880. This was to the age of 10, rising to 11 in 1893 and to 14 in 1918. Children came to Penmark village school from Aberthaw, Llancarfan and St. Athan until a school was opened there in 1888. The children at the vicarage and Castle usually had a governess.

A normal day at school started at 9:30am, there was a break for lunch at 12:30 and the day closed with Prayers and a hymn at 4pm. When the teacher was ill or on business, the school was closed.

Holidays followed the church calendar. On Ascension Day, school finished at 11 am, when the children attended a church service before going home. There was a whole day holiday on each of Ash Wednesday, Good Friday, Easter Monday and Whit Monday and a week at Christmas. St. David's day holiday was introduced in 1900, allowing staff and pupils to attend the singing festival in Cardiff, although no Welsh was spoken in school. Also, there were four weeks holiday in mid August to mid September, referred to as the Harvest holiday, and a half day for the fair in mid April.

Apart from the days allowed for holidays and closures of the school when it was being cleaned, whitewashed or repaired or the closets emptied, there were numerous absences of children from school and it is a recurring theme in the records that it was difficult to get the children to attend. Seasonal agricultural activities influenced the attendances of the children, so that for example, in July there would be fewer children in school than usual, some being sick, others haymaking or staying at home whilst their parents were haymaking, whereas in October, many children would be away, engaged in drawing potatoes and in springtime they were working in the gardens or employed picking stones. Small attendance due to severe weather was a regular entry especially in times of heavy rains or snow. The school was closed for a week in February 1888 because of snow and there was another heavy fall in March of that year and the next two years. There were heavy snows in January 1895; only sixteen children arrived and these children were sent home. Miss Gregory started at the school in 1916. She cycled from Llanbethery but was unable to arrive in March when the roads were blocked with

24. *Penmark School Pupils 1927.*

snow and fallen trees. In September 1918 there were floods and again Miss Gregory was not able to attend. In April 1920 the roads were blocked for days by a heavy fall of snow. Attendance of the children at school was very variable, any unusual outside event seemed to be more attractive. Generally, the children were easily distracted from school activities, they were noisy and not very studious. The main punishment was to keep them in after school. Children would be late in the afternoon through watching a funeral, staying to see the sheep washed or due to some more interesting recreation at the sea. Some just failed to return after lunch! If the hunt was in the area on a Friday, the boys would leave school to follow it and take their punishment on the Monday. In May 1869 there was a small attendance at school in consequence of a meeting at the Dissenters Chapel. In August 1898, several companies of Church lads brigade were camping in the area for three days, so the school was closed.

The report of H.M.Inspector in 1863 said "the attendance is below average, many of the children being employed in fieldwork. There has been some improvement since last year. Religious knowledge, reading and dictation in the first class are fair, but further attention should be given to writing and arithmetic and the discipline should be more strictly upheld. One boy shows considerably higher attainment than the rest".

In May there were 52 names on the school's register but only 20 were present. The Vicar examined 14 children in arithmetic

>   2 practise
>   4 compound multiplications
>   6 simple multiplications
>   3 simple addition

Only Elizabeth Thomas and William Deere did all the work without a mistake.

The working day consisted of reading, scripture, arithmetic, singing and sewing for girls. The vicar visited daily to teach scripture, often accompanied by his wife. His daughter sometimes went to supervise sewing or music. Mr and Mrs O.H. Jones visited on occasions.

H.M.Inspector reported that the school continues to make fair progress although some difficulty is felt owing to the small attendance of scholars during summer months. Further efforts are needed in order to obtain more correct spelling and improved tone and expression in reading.

In September 1864 there were 40 pupils present, with 5 new girls when a Geography lesson was given by the Master on The Map Of The World. In February 1865, Mr George Glover was appointed as the new master. The Inspector reported that the school on the whole was in fair condition but the instruction was not much advanced. It was hoped that the new master would improve the standard. No children had been presented for examination and attendance was very irregular. It was suggested that pre-payment of fees with discount for long periods would improve attendance. It was queried why the schoolmaster did not live in the schoolhouse provided on the ground floor. He in fact rented out the property and kept the rent !

The report for 1866 noted that attendance had improved, progress in other respects was fair and gave the opinion that the school, in time, was likely to obtain an average standard. The Master must have impressed because in 1867 "there was an improvement in all aspects, the master worked with energy and with a fair success. Results were

25. *Miss Thomas at Higher End 1930's.*

creditable, with the exception of arithmetic in the fifth standard". In July of 1867, Mr George Passmore became the new master. Attendance was low as they had been without a master for two weeks. This man put great emphasis on the catechism, which pupils learned by rote and was more severe in punishing any latecomers. At this time there were 50 children on the school register. A school clock and pictures were put up but the Inspector was not impressed by the new Headmaster. In 1869 the report for arithmetic was very unfavourable, money was deducted from the grant and Mr Passmore's certificate as master deferred until "he produces more favourable results". Three weeks later, Mr Arthur commenced duties as master ! He recorded that the noise from the children was too great a hindrance to the work of the school and the children needed better discipline. Several children were kept in for their conduct.

In 1872 the H.M.I. report stated "where scholars of both sexes attend above the age of infants, the offices must be separate and provided with separate means of access from the schoolroom itself, otherwise the whole grant forfeited." At that time there were 68 children registered at the school.

In 1877 the report stated that the school was backward, especially in arithmetic and suggested that the walls should be redecorated. The room itself should be kept in a somewhat tidier state and all useless articles removed. Even the arrangement of the desks was considered to be inconvenient and that they should be placed in parallel rows side by side. Also a good map of Europe was needed.

The attendance officer is first mentioned in 1878 when he "took the names of irregular children". Mr. Richards, the school master, died suddenly on July 24th. His daughter, Mary Penelope, who held a government certificate second class, was appointed principal teacher pro tem. The school was washed during the holidays. Fifteen new slates were received and there were 70 children on the roll.

Matilda Hopkin, a monitor in 1880, was asked to learn her lessons over again, so she went home. The managers asked her to apologise, but she refused and was dismissed. She was followed by Janetta West from Northampton as pupil teacher. She lodged with the Thomas family at Higher End who were a shoemaking family employing three men. Janetta was presented with a silver watch when she left in November 1882 after obtaining a scholarship and completing her apprenticeship.

In April 1885, the head teacher was away and her brother was again in charge. Seven children were late arriving at school; they said they did not know the time and he suggested it might be useful to have a school bell. In October that year, when many came to school "drenched to the skin" he suggested a fire would not be amiss. In June 1885, David Richards became headmaster and closed the school for two weeks to allow the children to work at the harvest. The school received 6 historical readers, some foolscap and blotting paper. In October, the duties of David Richards ceased and Elizabeth Williams took over as head teacher. A fire was lit on October 23rd. The average attendance was down to 32.

In July 1886, Libby Aubrey was asked to help with the infants whilst the pupil teacher went to Bristol for a scholarship examination. In August many of the younger children were absent from school with skin disease. This year the songs approved were

26. *The Cottage c.1925 with village children.*

1) O come come away
2) The clock
3) Stitch Stitch
4) Ring the bell watchman
5) Catch the sunshine
6) Boat song
8) Bugle home

Infants
1) Little dolly
2) Cock sparrow
3) Sing a song of sixpence
4) We'll all stand up together,

Harriet Hopkin, sister of Matilda commenced as monitor. The Inspector stated that there was a falling-off in quality and quantity in elementary work and scarcely any evidence of efficient teaching. When Rosa Nurton became head in 1888, she thought the standards very poor, work was untidy, reading monotonous and writing defective throughout. New books and T squares were supplied. In April, Mary and John Jenkins returned to school after nearly three months absence. In November, Ethel Howell became monitor but left after three months.

Rosa Nurton resigned in May 1890 and was replaced by Frederick Duck. He was appointed on 5th May 1890 and served for nearly forty years. He was well suited to his task and his efforts led to a steady improvement in standards over many years. There were then 63 children in the school and a ticket system was introduced to try to encourage regular attendance for which prizes would be given.

Mister Duck is a very good man
He goes to church on Sunday
He prays to God to give him strength
To whip the kids on Monday.

In December the children were entertained to a magic lantern show and prizes were distributed by Mr O. Jones to children who had been most regular during 1892. That was the year in which Leonora Thomas from Higher End became assistant mistress and stayed for over thirty years. The Headmaster, Mr Duck married her sister in 1893.

Progress was soon noted by the Inspectors who classed the school as good, with improvements in all areas. "However, some of the children are very old for the classes in which they are taught because they are not sent to school early enough". They now criticised the school building, stating the need for a classroom for the infants or possibly new premises. It was considered that an area of 517 square yards including playground was sufficient for 99 children, implying an inefficient use of floor space. This led to a meeting at the school in February 1894 between H.M.Inspector, the Vicar and an architect.

In May 1895 a contract for alterations to the school building was given to Mr James. After taking measurements he "set about the work without delay, starting on offices and other exterior alterations". The cost, including architect's fees (Mr Carter of Cardiff)

27. *School certificate – Fanny Prosser 1896.*

was £240. The walls were panelled using the old pews from the church, the outer steps and first floor were removed and a gallery was constructed at the east end with stairs going to it. For this work to proceed, the school was closed for five weeks.

The subsequent report of H.M.I. said that "it had been immensely improved and is now most satisfactory. When funds are available an endeavour should be made to provide new desks for the children". During the Easter holiday of 1896 the school was re-coloured and desks of the latest design were installed. The cost was considerably over £25. During the summer holiday in 1920 the school was completely renovated. The gallery was removed and the bell rope lengthened. The small playground 60 foot by 20 foot was divided, with girls and boys segregated, and separate toilets in each section. Further repairs to the school were carried out in 1925 under the instruction of the school managers. The boys' playground was cemented and the roof and door of the boys' lavatories and the lobby ceiling were repaired.

In 1896, it was decided that the abstract method of teaching arithmetic would be discontinued and a suitable book of progress would be provided. Mental arithmetic would occasionally be given instead of crayon colouring which was no longer a compulsory subject. In December a lecture on temperance was given to the children. Physical Exercises were introduced the following year - to be undertaken on Friday afternoons. It was obvious that rain much affected attendance especially of those children who had the long walk from Aberthaw; when they arrived "soaking wet" there was little chance of their clothes drying although socks were hung to dry by the fires at each end of the building. These were lit by Mrs Price, who with her husband was appointed caretaker in 1900. The boys took it in turns to carry the coal and also to go to the well for water, although by now there was a single tap at the rear of the school supplied from a rain water tank above the back entrance. In 1900 Miss Thomas spent 2 days at Palmeston infants school as the new teaching methods employed there would be introduced at Penmark. Cottage gardening was introduced for older children at the school and land opposite the school was offered by O.H. Jones for a school garden. This was managed by the boys who grew mainly vegetables. Older girls took part in a Doll Dressing competition in connection with Cardiff Bazaar in aid of waifs and strays. Anne Murphy and Mary Watts each won a prize of three shillings.

In January 1901 a tea party was thrown for Rev. Morgan who was leaving. Proceedings were brought to a close on hearing of the death of Queen Victoria. Later that year occasional walks were arranged in the hope that the children would grow up to take an intelligent interest in the common things connected with rural life and industries and a calendar of wild flowers was hung on the wall. The following year, the Inspector recommended that some separation should be made between the infant class and the older children. Mr James was asked to erect a partition during the Easter holiday. This was extended up to the ceiling eight years later.

There were 71 children registered at the school in 1903; the Inspector stated there were insufficient staff and the infant accommodation was limited. A year later the number registered had risen to 82.

In 1907 Elizabeth Bowen was presented by managers with a silver watch and chain for regular attendance, as reported on June 30 in the Barry Dock News "Lillie Bowen was admitted to Penmark school in 1900 and left in 1907 having attended without being once absent or late".

In 1912 H.M. Inspector reported that a satisfactory feature of the school is the care

28. *Group of children outside the school possibly VE celebrations.*

with which work is done. Penmanship is well taught. The rural character of the surroundings is recognised, gardening taught to older boys and some nature lessons are given to all the children, but teaching in English, geography, history and arithmetic is rather too bookish. It was noted that overcrowding had been relieved by exclusion of the under 5's.

In 1925 Miss Gregory resigned and was replaced by Miss Crowther.

The vicar, as chairman of the managers, addressed the scholars on the advantages of punctual and regular attendance and gave prizes to the following

6 years	Michael and Nelly Bryan
2 years	Thomas Bryan and Marjory Vizard
1 year	Sarah Wiltshire, Tom Roberts, D.West
	Leslie Butcher, James Bryan, Ruby Verrall.

In Sept 1928 Miss Crowther resigned to enter Barry Technical college. The average attendance for the year was recorded as 93.3% perhaps due to the attendance officer who visited weekly.

Miss Thomas's activities as supplementary teacher ended when she resigned in 1929. The managers wished to place on record their appreciation of her services for 36 years and invited past and present scholars to co-operate with them in providing a Testimonial to mark the termination of her services. £21 was collected and this was presented at a social evening held in the schoolroom.

The school log book has an entry at March 31st 1930 recording the resignation of the Headmaster Mr Duck after 39 years and 11 months of service. The following day his place was taken by Mr H.N. Rees with Valma Amelia Jean Jones as the uncertified teacher. She left the following year to return to Gower and Miss Griffiths was appointed in her place. She also stayed only for a few months and Miss E.J. Edmunds was transferred from Porthkerry school. Mr Duck's resignation was a sad episode in the history of the school, as he was hoping to continue as head until the school closed. However, the Education committee informed the Managers at the end of 1929 that they were adopting the resolution that all teachers over 60 years of age and with 40 years service were to retire in the following March. The managers stressed that the new school was being built but the Authorities said strict adherence to the resolution would be enforced and so Mr Duck had to leave. He died seven months later aged 62. His wife died in 1959 aged 92 years.

In July 1930 the assistant county librarian came to enquire as to whether books were being used by adults and a notice board was erected to inform people of the facilities.

In 1931 Thomas William Roberts was the first pupil to win a scholarship to Barry County school. William Rees gained an entrance scholarship. The following year Nina Wiltshire was granted a free scholarship having gained 237/300 marks.

The school log book for February 9th 1933 records

> "School closed by order of the local Education Authority. Penmark children will now attend the new council school at Rhoose. Miss E.J. Edmunds is being transferred to the school on February 13th."

February 10th found H.N. Rees and Miss Edmunds supervising the transfer of

LOT 15.

ALL THAT

Desirable Freehold Semi-Detached
Villa Residence

With Large Garden, situate in

PENMARK VILLAGE,

and adjoining the premises belonging to the Calvinistic Methodist Chapel,

Now in the occupation of Mr. F. DUCK (on a weekly tenancy).

(Coloured Blue on the Sale Plan No. 3.)

The house contains on the Ground Floor, two sitting rooms, Kitchen and Scullery, and on the first floor, four bedrooms.

The purchaser of this Lot will be required to block up any access to the adjoining land.

LOT 16.

ALL THAT

Desirable Semi-Detached Freehold
Dwelling House

Adjoining the above, and at present let to the GLAMORGAN COUNTY COUNCIL as a Police Station on a quarterly tenancy determinable by notice as from 30th May, and subsequent quarter days.

(Coloured Brown on the Sale Plan No. 3.)

The house contains on the Ground Floor, two Sitting Rooms, Kitchen, and Scullery, and has a good Conservatory at the rear. On the First Floor are four Bedrooms.

The purchaser of this Lot will be required to block up any access to the adjoining land.

29.   *Auction 1917 – homes of policeman and headmaster.*

furniture, books etc. to Rhoose School. Mr Rees resumed his duties at Dinas Powis School. Average attendance for the week 37.3 = 84.7%.

The administration of the school buildings and other financial aspects became the responsibility of the school managers in the early part of this century. The members were chosen from the Parish Council usually with the vicar chairing their meetings. The proposal in 1918 for a new school at Fonmon Cross was regretted by the managers but they recognised that with the increased population in Aberthaw and Rhoose a more central school was necessary. They said that they would offer no opposition provided that the present staff were retained and thought a site nearer Nurston would be more suitable. In 1913 they decided that the closets should be emptied at Christmas and midsummer and not three times a year as recommended! By the time the school closed, this had been increased to four times a year.

Purchases by them included a new stove and football, a blind for the south window and hall pegs.

In 1928 the County Council suggested the following improvements:-

> Overhead covering for the playground, improved lighting and a separate lavatory for the teachers.

The managers' response was that the playground was too small to cover, the lighting was sufficient and separate lavatories were unnecessary. They were however overruled on the last point, so they compromised by taking one from the boy's side and one from the girls and providing a lock and key.

HEALTH

We forget today how serious were the consequences of illness in the days before antibiotics. The school log book records vividly the incidence of childhood diseases and the steps taken to control the spread of infection. In October 1883, the school was closed for three weeks because of fever; the Education Department was notified and a doctor was sent to get details of all affected children. Aberthaw children were not allowed to attend until December. Again, in October two years later, many were away because of whooping cough and in June 1887 there was scarlet fever at Aberthaw, so no children from that village were allowed to attend. There was an outbreak of measles in December 1888 and the following August the school was closed for ten days because of whooping cough and a suspected case of diphtheria. The medical authorities closed the school in December 1891 owing to the number of children suffering from scarlet fever and it remained closed for seven weeks. Even so, Aberthaw children were still ill five months later and by then ten Penmark children had mumps. Miss Thomas was also absent as the fever was in her house and the school was again closed in July, this time for five weeks. An outbreak of whooping cough in 1899 caused the school to be closed a week early for the holidays and it remained closed for seven weeks. By September the epidemic was over, but chickenpox and diphtheria continued until February, when the school was again closed. In 1904, three children with scarlet fever had to stay away for six weeks and twenty two children were excluded from school with chicken pox.

30. *Policeman c.1856 (kind permission of Bridgend Police Museum).*

Influenza struck in March 1908, whooping cough followed in July together with a measles epidemic which closed the school. Ten years later, the school was again closed for two weeks because of influenza and again in 1920 because of measles and whooping cough. After a german measles epidemic in 1931, two boys and one girl were recommended for Pendine open air camp.

The school nurse was first mentioned in 1915 when she examined the clothing of all the children and by 1920 she was visiting monthly, often accompanied by a doctor. The school dental surgeon first appeared in 1924. In that year, the older children were lectured on tuberculosis by Mr Owen Williams and again ten years later by Miss Edith Rowlands. An entry in the school log book for 1931 evokes strong feelings

> "County dentist and a nurse attended all day and 29 children received extractions and fillings."

There were sixty further treatments over the following weeks.

Death was no stranger in the parish and it was then that the "handywoman" was called for. She was usually a motherly figure who saw one into the world and saw one out of the world. Her primary role in the mid-nineteenth century was that of midwife and she played a very important role in the community. Legislation was introduced in 1902 under which, officially, no uncertified person could deliver a child. Although not qualified, doctors in rural areas continued to allow them to work alongside registered midwives. They themselves had to be paid and were seldom called for childbirth. Usually, only married ladies were dealt with and unmarried girls "went away". Sometimes the workhouse was their only place of refuge.

The census of 1841 records Ann David, age 69, as a midwife and in 1909 there were three registered midwives, Jane John in St Athan and Adelaide Dunnett and Elizabeth Spiller in Rhoose.

Penmark's handywoman was Sarah Vizard, born in 1862 in Gileston. She lived on Barren Hill and brought up six children of her own. She died in 1946 and there are many people alive today whom she brought into the world. As legislation took over, she did more laying out than delivering. William, her husband, was a parish councillor for many years and was often employed by them to repair stiles and footpaths. He may also have been the gravedigger, a job which his son Fred is remembered for (as well as for having the first motorbike in the village).

In 1922 the parish council suggested a public meeting with Porthkerry Council for the purpose of engaging a district nurse. One was appointed and in 1939 a clinic was opened in Rhoose.

The earliest Doctor remembered by villagers was Dr King from Barry. When he was needed someone had to ride out to fetch him, but many would be reluctant to do this and rely instead on herbal remedies, poultices etc.

POLICE FORCE

The County Police Force Act of 1839 enabled boroughs to establish a police force. Prior to this, a Constable was appointed at the vestry meeting to keep the peace locally and to arrest anyone disturbing it. This was an unpaid position and usually passed around

PENMARK is a parish and village, 3 miles north-west from Barry station on the Great Western railway, 12 south-west from Cardiff and 6 south-east from Cowbridge, in the Southern division of the county of Glamorgan, Dynas Powis hundred, St. Nicholas petty sessional division, Cardiff union and county court district, rural deanery of Llandaff Lower (western division) and archdeaconry and diocese of Llandaff. The extension of the Taff Vale railway from Cowbridge through this parish to Abertbaw, which is a hamlet in this parish, is now (1891) in course of construction. The church of St. Mary is a building of stone in the Gothic style, consisting of chancel with aisle, nave, south porch and an embattled western tower containing 6 bells: there are 150 sittings, of which 115 are free. The register of baptisms and burials dates from the year 1750; marriages, 1756; but is in a bad state of preservation. The living is a vicarage, commuted tithe rent-charge £230, average £174, net yearly income £225, including 100 acres of glebe and residence, in the gift of the Dean and Chapter of Gloucester, and held since 1844 by the Rev. Charles Frederick Bryan Wood M.A. of Pembroke College, Oxford, and precentor of Llandaff cathedral. There is a Welsh Calvinistic chapel. The principal charities are derived from the rent of two cottages, 2½ acres of land and the interest on £62 10s. distributed on the Thursday before Easter to poor persons not in receipt of parish relief, by the vicar and churchwardens, who are the trustees. Near the church are the ruins of an ancient castle, built soon after the Norman Conquest by one of the Umfrevilles. Fonmon Castle is the seat of Oliver Henry Jones esq. J.P. who is the lord of the manor. Halswell Melborne Keneys-Tynte esq. J.P. of Cefn Mably and W. C. Rayer are the principal landowners. The soil is clay; subsoil, limestone. The chief crops are wheat, barley and oats. The area is 3,356 acres of land and 177 of foreshore; rateable value, £4,025; the population in 1891 was 548.

Abertbaw is a hamlet on the sea shore. There are lime kilns in this hamlet, the property of the Aberthaw Pebble Lime Co. Limited.

Fonmon, Fontygary, Rhoose, Tredogan, Burton and Nearstone are other hamlets in the parish: there is a Congregational chapel at Nearstone and a Baptist chapel at Aberthaw.

Parish Clerk, Henry David.

Post Office.—John Alexander, postmaster. Letters through Cowbridge at 9 a.m. & dispatched at 3.30 p.m. The nearest money order & telegraph office is at Barry

National School, Frederick Duck, schoolmaster

[Letters for names marked thus * are received through Barry, Cardiff.]

Jones Olvr. Hy. J.P. Fonmon castl. Fonmon
Wood Rev. Charles Frederick Bryan M.A. The Vicarage

COMMERCIAL.

*Aberthaw Pebble Lime Co. Lim. Aberthw
Alexander John, grocer & postmaster

Aubrey Edward, Six Bells P.H
Bowen Mary (Mrs.), farmer
Harbottle Thomas, farmer, Fonmon
*Harry Thomas, Carpenters' Arms P.H. Whitehall
Hopkin Thomas, Red Cow P.H
James Wm. farmer & carpenter, Fonmon
*James John, farmer, Blackton farm

Jenkins Edward, farmer, Penmark pl
*Jenkins William, farmer, Rhoose
Jones Matthew, Rose & Crown P.H
*Jones Mrs. farmer, Tredogan
*Liscombe Lewis, Blue Anchor P.H. Aberthaw
*Lougher James, farmer, Aberthaw
*Matthews Thomas, farmer, Fontygary

31. Trade Directory 1891.

amongst parishioners, in other words, parish officers were responsible for keeping law and order. The Glamorgan Constabulary was formed in 1841. Captain Charles Napier was the first Chief Constable and had 34 officers under him.

The first policeman known to have been in the village was Charles Rodman who was 27 when he was stationed here in 1857. He came from Gloucester. It was not unusual for the police to be recruited from the agricultural labourers as they were familiar with the ways of country folk. From Penmark, Charles Rodman moved to Cardiff, St Brides, Newton Nottage, Mountain Ash and Merthyr Tydfill where by 1881 he had reached the rank of Inspector.

Policemen serving in the Penmark Police House, with place of birth where known were:

YEAR	NAME	BIRTHPLACE
1857	Charles Rodman	Gloucester
1859	Charles Smith	
1861	George Maybury	Berkshire
1864	George Perkins	Somerset,
1869	John Beer	Devon
1881	Frederick Daggs	Cardiff.
1885	Arthur Davies	Pembroke.
1896	Henry Headon	
1905	John Williams	
1913	Charles Lewis	
1922	William Saunders	
1925	Leonard Norman	
1935	Alfred Jones	
1939	Mr Ryan	
1940	Penryth Davies	
1945	Mr Hargreaves	

The police records for 1900 describe Arthur Davies as being 6 feet 1 and a half inches tall, fresh complexion, brown hair, blue eyes with a scar on his forehead and moles on his face. In February 1890, he was disciplined for neglect of duty in not arresting supposed fowl thieves.

The appearance of the early policeman was quite striking. His uniform consisted of a blue swallow-tailed coat with a leather collar and large inside pockets for handcuffs, whistle and staff. The trousers were white in summer, blue in winter and the hat was tall.

Penmark Police House was vacated in 1954 and Mr Hargreaves went to a newly built police house in Rhoose. Penmark Police house is marked at the top of Barren Hill, opposite Well Lane on the 1879 map and also in a 1917 document where it is referred to as Old Police Station. I believe it remained there until a new house was built in 1908 which is now used as the post office.

PENMARK, VALE OF GLAMORGAN

Situate quite near to Rhoose Airport

Messrs. JOHN DAVID, WATTS & MORGAN have received instructions to SELL BY AUCTION at THE SIX BELLS HOTEL, PENMARK, on WEDNESDAY, DECEMBER 2nd, 1959 at 7.30 p.m.
(Subject to Conditions of Sale to be then read)

THE VALUABLE FREEHOLD DWELLING HOUSE AND BUSINESS PREMISES
known as

The Old Post Office, Penmark

Containing :

SHOP ; THREE ROOMS DOWN AND PANTRY ; THREE BEDROOMS ; BOX ROOM ; BATHROOM AND TOILET

Outside :

LARGE GARDEN AT REAR. YARD ON SIDE. STONE AND SLATE-ROOF STABLE ; STONE AND SLATE-ROOF SHED now let to Mr. Walsh and which could be used as Garage.

Mains Water. Electric Light.

Rateable Value £19.

VACANT POSSESSION (with exception of Shed let to Mr. Walsh) will be given upon completion.

Also will be included in the Sale :

The Freehold Cottage now let at 14/- per week, known as

Rose Cottage, Penmark

BRICK AND STONE-BUILT with SLATE ROOF, containing TWO ROOMS DOWN and TWO BEDROOMS. Outside there is a STONE and PANTILED ROOF SHED with side access, which could be used as a Garage. OUTSIDE TOILET.

Water and Electric Light.

Further particulars and orders to view may be obtained from the Auctioneers at Cowbridge (Tel. 242) and Bridgend (Tel. 61), or from Messrs. J. A. Hughes & Co., Solicitors, Holton Road, Barry Dock.

Printed by D. Brown & Sons Ltd., Cowbridge, Glamorgan

Auction 1959.

FIRE SERVICE

It is hard to realise now that it was only in 1938 that Parliament passed legislation allowing each district to make provision for extinguishing fires and the protection of life and property in the case of fire. Prior to this, payment had to be made each time a fire appliance was called out, and unless summoned by an "authorised person", it could not be used.

In 1924 Porthkerry Council asked if Penmark would assist in the upkeep of a fire appliance which had been used for fires in that parish. An annual payment of £2-2-0 was agreed provided that

1) it shall be available when needed and
2) the sum can be withdrawn any time if the council so decide.

Twelve months later, another meeting was held with Porthkerry Council to discuss the offer of Barry fire engine and this they started to use in 1926. The agreed charge (on six months notice) for the use of the Barry fire engine was £12 for the first hour and £6 for subsequent hours. The authorised person for calling up the brigade was to be the police officer stationed in Penmark. The Council took out insurance with the British Oak Insurance Co. covering its liability to £100, with £20 maximum for one attendance and no more than 5 calls per year. The premium for this was £5 per annum.

It was soon realised that as the parish was scattered, more people were needed to be responsible for calling the fire brigade and Mr James at Fonmon, Mr Nott at Rhoose and Mr Lougher at Aberthaw were authorised. In 1935 there was dispute about paying for the fire engine which had been called out by a non authorised person! In 1938 the authorised people were in Penmark Rev Williams, in Aberthaw John David, in Nurston W. Webb and in Fonmon Idris James plus Sir Seymour Boothby.

POST and TELEPHONE

According to a newspaper report in 1847, "Penmark was isolated in the Vale and unprovided with postal facilities." John Alexander at the Mount wrote to the Lord Lieutenant concerning this and on April 15th of that year he became the village's first sub-postmaster at a salary of £4 per annum. Henry Lewis, a single man living in Aberthin, was appointed postal messenger at 12/- per week. Post was delivered and despatched through Cowbridge and his route took him through St Hilary, Llantrithyd and Llancarfan. I believe that Lewis did his round on foot whilst the Llantwit Major messenger had a tricycle. They were both outdone by the rural letter carrier at St Athan who had a donkey! The letter carrier at the turn of the century was Joseph Smith who lived in Primrose Cottage (next door to the police station). By then a horse was the usual mode of transport, and an allowance was provided for the horse's keep. Mr. Alexander remained sub-postmaster for fifty years and was succeeded on his death by his son William who also lived at the Mount. The money order and telegraphic office was now at Barry and, in 1899, with the opening of the railway line, the post was also routed through there. Permission was given to establish a money order office in Penmark provided that the Council guaranteed the sum of £5 per annum, less the

33. Villagers watching the hunt.

amount of revenue derived from the business during the year. This they agreed to and in 1900 they also guaranteed £14 per year (binding for seven years) for the establishment of a Telegraph Office. The income received never reached £10 in any year, so the council paid the deficit.

In 1903, the clerk wrote to the Postmaster General asking how much would be paid annually provided six residents had private telephones. The reply stated that it was impossible to open an exchange unless the council agreed to modify their previous agreement, which they did not. There had been complaints a few years earlier that the water at Nurston had been rendered quite unfit for drinking purposes through the erection of a telephone post directly over the spring - progress had its problems!

In 1926 a GPO collection box was placed in Tredogan, but a request for one at Model Farm, Port Road was rejected.

William Thomas took over from William Alexander about 1906 and the post office moved to his home on the opposite side of the road, where many locals remember it. After he died, his wife Annie continued to run the post office until Mrs Roberts became sub-postmistress in the mid-thirties. Again the office crossed the road, and the post box which had once been in the window of the shop, was put into the wall of the Old Police House. The present site was established after the death of Mrs Roberts in 1959.

In 1928 the Council asked the Postmaster in Barry if the time of despatch of letters as well as the date could be stamped on them. They also complained that the post office opened too late, for if a letter received in the morning had to be replied to urgently, it could not be done as no stamp could be obtained in time for the morning collection. Also, no letters were delivered at Barren Hill in the evening. A later complaint stated that the 7.30 am delivery was not reaching its destination until 8.50 am.

In 1935 there was a request for phone boxes at Penmark and Aberthaw because the post offices closed at 7:00 pm. The phone was inside the shop in Penmark and one could sit down when using it.

SHOPS, PUBS and PEOPLE

William Thomas was already a wheelwright, carpenter, undertaker and carrier to Cardiff (Saturdays) when he took over the post office, his workshop was in the yard behind what is now Rose Cottage. His wife continued to run the shop known as the Old Post Office until she left the village in 1959 aged 92. She is remembered for "cutting sweets in half to get the correct weight!" Her retirement was spent living with relatives in Cardiff but she was brought back to be buried in the churchyard with her parents on her death at the age of 101. William when he died in 1928 was buried in Llancarfan chapel grounds with Catherine his first wife and three infant children.

John Alexander was involved in many activities and ran a thriving store and market garden from the many greenhouses and outbuildings at the Mount. "Grocer & dealer in sundries" according to the 1880 trade directory, but he was also subpostmaster, churchwarden and farmer. The Mount was referred to as "the market place" at the end of the century. It had been occupied by the Alexander family since 1845 but had been used as a shop continuously since at least 1760. According to his obituary, Mr Alexander was "of an antiquarian bent" and took a keen interest in the genealogy of

34.   Wheelwright and apprentice c.1920.

local families having "enjoyed the company of Iolo Morganwg in his younger days". He had been a lifelong Liberal, greatly admiring Mr Gladstone and was highly esteemed in the Village by both church people and non-conformists.

Captain Evans, a large bearded gentleman who intrigued the children because of his frequent "disappearances" to sea, bought the Mount from the Alexander family for his retirement home. Unfortunately he died on his last voyage and is buried in America. His widow Emily, who was born in the village and was living next door at Gileston House when they married, remained at the house until she died at the age of 86. She is buried with her parents and 20 members of her family in the churchyard. Her death in 1952 ended the Hopkin connection with the village which started in 1858. In that year Thomas Hopkin, son of Evan Hopkin, blacksmith of St Athan, brought his new bride to the Rose and Crown where he took over from the Gabriel family the role of blacksmith and publican. Four of their twelve children were born at Kenson before they moved to Fonmon, Thomas again working as a blacksmith. Their last child, Ada Louise, was born in 1880 when the family was back in Penmark, this time Thomas being publican at the Red Cow.

This ale house had had many owners, none of whom actually lived there. The deeds of 1823 refer to it as "a mansion, barn, garden and orchard" although it later became two dwellings, one being a pub, and the other the Police Station. In 1839 the dwelling house called The Stag Frigate was sold by Thomas Flanders to Mr Lougher. It was sold again in 1876 to P. Williams a brewer who renamed it The Red Cow, and sold it in 1886 to William Hancock. In 1907, John Jones, a retired victualler bought it and three years later sold it to George Moss, gentleman, who sold it two years later to Thomas Hopkin the man who had been publican for fifteen years. In 1895 Thomas became publican at the newly built Bassett Hotel in Barry but the family of at least nine people including grandchildren, continued to live in the property. The Red Cow ceased to be a pub in October 1907 and Thomas renamed it Gileston House - the name of the village where his wife was born. He died in 1913 leaving £7,000.

The only public house remaining in the village is the Six Bells. This like many surrounding properties is a 16th century building which was extensively refurbished in the 19th century and the only original part remaining is the central chamfered 4-centred doorway. The Aubrey family lived there for over forty years but again were not the owners. The property was sold on the 5th of April 1875 by William Evans of Merthyr Tydfil to David Evans of Cardiff, High Bailiff to the County court, for the sum of two hundred and eighty pounds. For this sum, David Evans received "all that messuage or dwellinghouse curtilage orchard and garden thereunto belonging and adjoining situate at Penmark in the said county of Glamorgan and now used as a public house by the name of the Six Bells and which said premises are now in the occupation of Edward Aubrey and also all that smiths forge adjoining the said last mentioned dwellinghouse and which has lately been converted into and is now used as a coachhouse to the said Public house".

35. *Preparing for the show c.1900.*

The publicans who served in Penmark Village were,

	RED COW	ROSE & CROWN (Kenson)	SIX BELLS
1841	Mary David	John Gabriel	Jane Williams
1854	Morris Griffiths	Will Jones	Jane Williams
1861	Morris Griffiths	Thomas Hopkin	John Evans
1865	John Evans	Will Harry	Edward Aubrey
1871	Sophia Curl	Catherine Harry	Edward Aubrey
1881	Thomas Hopkin	Matthew Jones	Edward Aubrey
1891	Thomas Hopkin	Matthew Jones	Edward Aubrey
1895	John Lester	John Dunscombe	Edward Aubrey
1901	John Lester	Thomas Wilcox	John Aubrey
1907	David Stew	William Williams	John Aubrey

The Aubrey occupancy was broken when John moved to a cottage in Barren Hill in 1917 and William Cannon became the landlord. He stayed for about twelve years and was followed by Mr. Williams and Bob Styles. Other public houses in the Parish were The Carpenters Arms at Whitehall (now the Highwayman) and The Blue Anchor and Malsters Arms at East Aberthaw.

FARMING

The climate of the area was favourable for grain crops including barley, oats and wheat and much of the produce went to market. Most farms had a few sheep, stock were reared for sale and there were some dairy cattle, making it an area of mixed farming. There was a weekly market at Llantwit Major and the cattle were walked there and back. An agricultural show for the Vale was held at Cowbridge each September.

> From Barry to Cowbridge and down to the sea.
> Vale of Glamorgan good farmers are we

The majority of the population was connected in some way with the land. Irish labourers came for the harvest as wages in the Vale were quite high. Many stayed in the area, becoming casual labourers doing hedging, ditching or stone-picking according to the season. Even the women would stone-pick with their children because they needed the money. They were hard-working and when the native youths moved to the industrial valleys for more money, they took their place and gradually became absorbed into the local community. In 1867, agricultural labourers earned 12/- per week with extra at harvest time. This had risen to 19/- in 1898 with 2/- per day at harvest for reapers with sickle and 1/- for women and boys working as binders. Food was included. Often they were employed on a yearly basis. They lived in small cottages one up one down and a privy at the top of the garden, every inch of which was cultivated. They usually kept a pig and sometimes hens. A pig was killed by villagers in rotation so that all could have meat fresh. No part was wasted. The larger families lived in small rented cottages with

NOTE.—Lots 12 and 13 will be offered together as one Lot. See General Remarks.

LOT 12.

(Coloured Pink on the Sale Plan No. 3.)

A PORTION OF THE VALUABLE

FREEHOLD FARM

Situate at Penmark in the County of Glamorgan, within four miles of the town of Barry, and about two miles from Rhoose and Aberthaw Stations, Vale of Glamorgan Railway, known as

PENMARK FARM,

Including the picturesque "PENMARK CASTLE RUINS" and Old Farm House,

Lately, with the following Lot, in the occupation of the Owner, the late Evan Williams, deceased, and containing in the whole

217½ Acres or thereabouts

of Rich productive Pasture and Arable Lands, as set out in the following Schedule:

No. on 25in. Ord. Map. 1900 Edition.	Description and Cultivation.	Acreage.	No. on 25in. Ord. Map. 1900 Edition.	Description and Cultivation.	Acreage.
156	Farm House and Cottage Garden, &c.	0.376	202	Pasture	7.246
158 pt.	Buildings and Yards and Rickyard, say	0.929	206		3.579
159	Orchard	0.201	203	Arable	12.814
160	Pasture	5.227	207	Do.	27.019
199	Do.	4.867	228	Do.	14.980
200 pt.	Do.	8.006	149	Pasture	1.437
198	Do.	2.289	148	Do.	0.875
205	Do.	3.286	147	Do.	0.595
234	Do.	1.351	153	Do.	11.406
233	Do.	6.105	172	Do.	1.685
232	Arable	8.186	152	Do.	2.300
248	Do.	11.799	150	Do.	1.451
231	Pasture	4.234	154	Wood	12.228
245	Do.	4.131	155	Ruins of Castle and Pasture	2.859
279	Do.	11.318	171	Pasture	20.265
277	Do.	10.689	297	Do.	2.046
201	Arable	8.422	298	Pasture and Wood	3.413
		91.416			126.198
					91.416
					217.614

THE FARM HOUSE is of modern construction, and contains: Convenient and commodious Dining Room, Kitchens, and out-door Offices and four capital Bedrooms.

There is a large and magnificent range of substantial and recently erected FARM BUILDINGS, providing ample accommodation for all Stock; with enclosed yards, large French Barn, and Water Storage connected with all main buildings.

Possession of the Dwelling House and the Field No. 160 on the Plan, with right of access through the Farm Yard, is reserved until May 2nd, and the Vendors also reserve the right to have a Sale by Auction of the Furniture and remaining Farming Stock on the Farm premises.

The Drainage is made on the most approved principle, and the sewage is carried to a concrete and cemented Outfall Pit with overflow, about 200 yards from the house and buildings.

There are also magnificent walled-in gardens with conservatories, etc., well stocked with fruit trees of the best respective kinds.

The Tithe Rent Charges on this and the next Lot amounted for the year 1916 to £72 13s. 0d.

For the purposes of the Sale the Tithe is apportioned at four-sevenths of the total payable to Lot 12 and three-sevenths to Lot 13.

The Land Tax is apportioned at £5 4s. 0d.

stone slab floors possibly covered with rag (peg) rugs. The furniture was very basic, consisting of table, chairs and a cupboard and most had two small bedrooms upstairs. Lighting was by candles or oil lamps and cooking was on a coal or stick range. The water had to be carried from the pump or well but outside many homes was a water butt or container to collect rainwater. Wash day took all day, the water had to be collected and then boiled in a large vessel called a copper. The cottage would be full of steam, either from that or the damp clothes hung around to dry. Flat irons were heated on the open fire. As mentioned earlier, conditions were anything but idyllic with many of the cottages in a dangerous state of repair with leaking roofs and foul closets.

The village people had to be good managers and self sufficient; mother made and repaired clothes, father mended shoes. Life was hard with long hours of outside work and wages which were barely enough to keep a family, hence the need to grow vegetables etc. A blind eye was often turned towards poaching; the produce was sometimes exchanged in the pub for a pint! Locals would also barter or sell their garden produce and the fruits of the hedgerows were regularly eaten according to season. Harvest was a time of hard work but also of great excitement, for the children especially, when the steam engine and threshing machine arrived. This was hired, as was the binder and huller for threshing clover. Everyone including the women helped at harvest and were rewarded with rough cider or tea whilst the children chased the rabbits as they ran out of the corn.

Farm servants, usually single men, often lived in stables or outbuildings and did the important jobs about the farm. If they were in charge of the horses, it was not unusual for them to sleep with them. Sons and daughters of farm labourers often went into service in the farms where their parents worked.

The principal farms in Penmark village were Penmark Place, where the Jenkins family lived for most of the last century and Penmark Farm, where Joseph Bowen took his new bride in 1845. He died tragically in 1869 and is buried at Llantrisant with his two infant children. His eldest son Thomas, was farming until the end of the century, when he sold much of the land to Evan Williams, publican of the Victoria Hotel in Barry. Mrs Bowen continued to live at the farmhouse and was over 80 when she died in 1906. Her youngest son, Richard, married Margaret Aubrey, daughter of the publican at the Six Bells in 1892 and his descendants are still in the farmhouse today. Mr Williams was responsible for building outhouses on his land for the trotting horses he bred. These buildings later became barns and have recently been converted into houses. When the farm buildings were completed, he employed the masons to build a terrace of houses on land between the church and chapel. The first and last would be gabled, with smaller ones between but the work was stopped after only two houses had been completed. These were occupied by the schoolmaster and the policeman. When his properties were auctioned in 1917 they were bought by the Radcliffe Estate which owned the adjoining lands. The new tenants of the farms were William Rees and Emlyn Radcliffe; descendants of both men now own these farms.

Other farms in the parish were Blackton, Whitelands, Welford, New, Cringallt, Fonmon and Tredogan.

As machinery began to appear on the farms, fewer workers were needed although manual labour was still needed for hedging and ditching and repairing the roads. The cement works opened at Aberthaw in 1913 and had a marked effect on life in the area although there had been some quarrying prior to that.

37. Aberthaw Station.

DEVELOPMENT of TRANSPORT

Aberthaw had been an important port since Roman times and farm produce was exported from there in the 17th century. Many of the vessels sailed mainly along the Bristol Channel, but some went as far as the West Indies. One important commodity transported in large quantities was limestone to Devon and Somerset as it had special qualities for building material. Horse wagons were used by local farmers to collect chemicals such as lime and phosphate from Pleasant Harbour at Aberthaw before it was loaded onto boats. These farmers would also collect truck loads of coal for their home use which had been brought there by train. In summer, there was heavy passenger trade with men from the south west coming for harvesting. As with the Irish, many married local girls and stayed in the area.

The Vale of Glamorgan railway linking Barry to Bridgend was opened in December 1897. Now it was quick and easy to transport surplus milk and other market produce to Merthyr and the mining villages and hastened the change in the agricultural and social habits of the area. It also took local men from the land to the industrial areas. In 1922 this railway was merged into the Great Western with trains leaving Aberthaw from the upper station, serving Barry, Rhoose, Aberthaw, Gileston, Llantwit Major and Wick to Bridgend and the lower line to Cowbridge, Taff Vale, Pontyclun and Llantrisant.

A far from adequate bus service was available in 1925 run by Mr Griffiths. Vain attempts were made by the Parish Council to improve this service and to provide bus shelters for waiting passengers. After residents were asked which day and time would be suitable, Messrs White and Co. were asked to provide a service mid-week. In 1930 Messrs Blakemore and Vizard met Llancarfan Council to try to improve the bus services for both villages. A bus shelter was provided at Tredogan Cross in 1937.

Blacksmiths, apart from making horseshoes, repaired farm equipment and with the wheelwright, made the cartwheels so essential to village life. Although there were a number of thatched cottages there was no thatcher living in Penmark but there were tilers and carpenters. Lodging with the Vizards in 1891 was Frederick Howard, a mole catcher. These people were used on the farms mainly in winter. They used to set traps and called each day to empty them. The animal skins were pegged out to dry, then they were sold

The self sufficiency of the village is apparent from the occupations noted in the census returns. In 1841 there were 6 shopkeepers, 3 publicans, 3 farmers, 2 millers, 2 blacksmiths, 2 carpenters a shoemaker and a tiler. The chart shows that the population of the village has remained almost the same for 150 years. Of the 193 people in the village in 1841 only 14 had been born outside Glamorgan.

NAME and Surname of each Person	RELATION to Head of Family	CONDITION as to Marriage	AGE last Birthday of Males / Females	PROFESSION or OCCUPATION	Employer	Employed	Neither	WHERE BORN
Ellen Bridel	Servant	S	/ 18	Domestic Servant		X		Walsh Glam
David Power	Head	M	34	Agricultural Labour		X		Penmark
Margaret	Wife	M	/ 34					Conwill Elvet
Charles	Son	S	3 /					Llancarfan G
Mary	Daughter	S	/ 1					Penmark
William Mahn	Head	M	69	No occupation				Ireland
Julia	Wife	M	/ 55					Ireland
Florence Mahoney	Head	M	66 /	Farm Servant		X		Ireland
Catherine	Wife	M	/ 60					Ireland
John	Son	M	34	Farm Servant				Penmark Gl
Henry Harding	Head	M	37	Baptist Missionary	X			Somersetshire
Mary Jane	Wife	M	/ 32					Monmouthshire
Hubert	Son	S	4					Glamorganshire
Ernest Victor	Son	S	1					"
Matthew Jones	Head	Widr	73	Publican			X	"
Annie Morgan	Servant	S	/ 25	Domestic Servant		X		"
Janet Jeffries	"	S	/ 20					"
Edward Hulsey	Head	Widr	76	Publican			X	Slan
John	Son	S	34					"
Harriett	Daughter	S	/ 30					"
Margaret A.	"	S	/ 28					"
Eliza M.	"	S	/ 26					"
Ida G.	"	S	/ 22					B
Maud Churchill	Grand-daughr	S	/ 8					Brighton Sussex
William Thomas	Head	M	40	Carpenter & Wheelwright	X			Llancarvan G
Catherine R.	Wife	M	/ 36					St Lythians
Gertrude R.	Daughter	S	/ 10	Scholar				Penmark
William L.	Son	S	8					"
William Davies	Relative	S	70	Carpenter		X		Tymewydd
Evan D. Lewis	Boarder	S	36	Baptist Minister				Carmarthen
Total of Males and Females...			15 / 15					

38. Census 1891 (Crown copyright).

Crown Copyright material in the Public Record Office is reproduced by permission of the Controller of Her Majesty's Stationery Office.

PEOPLE and HOUSES

	Male	Female	Child	House	Persons
1841	72	79	42	53	193
1851	71	71	79	44	221
1881	63	60	56	43	179
1891	63	56	53	48	172
1995	54	58	35	58	147

OCCUPATIONS

Year	1841	1851	1861	1871	1881	1891
Miller	2	1	1	1	-	-
Carrier	-	-	3	2	1	1
Publican	3	3	3	3	3	3
Shoemaker	-	4	2	3	4	-
Farmer	2	4	2	3	4	4
Teacher	-	1	1	1	2	2
Butcher	-	-	1	1	2	3
Shopkeeper	6	2	3	2	1	2
Blacksmith	2	2	2	1	1	3
Carpenter	3	2	2	2	2	3
Policeman	-	1	1	1	1	1
Ag. lab.	18	15	20	32	12	19
Tiler	1	2	1	1	1	-
Cleric	1	1	1	1	1	2
Servant	15	16	14	1	9	26
Charwoman	-	-	1	-	3	3
Mason	-	2	1	4	1	3
Gardener	-	2	2	2	1	-
Dressmaker	-	4	2	2	3	2
Tailor	-	2	1	1	1	-
Coachman	-	-	-	-	1	-

Throughout the last century the village was not only self-sufficient, but was the "shopping centre" for the surrounding villages. From the 1891 census we find that Alexander Thomas at Higher End as well as being a shoemaker, farmer, the father of the school mistress and father in law of the school master, was also a butcher. These "occupations" he still had in 1905. Other butchers in the village were William Watts

39. *Bowen brothers outside Penmark Farm c.1890.*

senior and junior and James Ford. I do not know which properties the latter occupied, but it is known that the buildings at the side of the Croft were used as slaughter houses. The large greenhouses at the Mount were in constant use into this century and the last shoemaker Alexander Thomas, was still working at Higher End following his father and grandfather. The latter had come into the village from West Wales during the first years of the 19th century and lived to be over 90. Longevity was not uncommon in the Parish, with many people living to be over 80. In the 20th century, both Annie Thomas and Alice Jones reached 100 years of age.

Although there were still two shops here in the 1950's run by Mrs Thomas and Mrs Evans, the way of life had been gradually changing over many years. With the arrival of the railway it was possible to go to Cardiff or Bridgend for luxuries which had formerly been bought from the travelling packman. It still meant walking to Rhoose for the train or harnessing the trap to go to Barry. Bicycles were another form of transport, and in some cases tricycles. Milk was available from the farms but daily tradesmen began to call including Kerslake the baker from Barry, Wagstaff the oilman and Murrin the butcher on his bike.

CONCLUSION

Although there have been enormous social and economic changes in the last century, the layout of Penmark village has hardly altered. One can imagine a walk through the village in 1895, approaching down the hill from Llancarfan. First we pass a small cottage on the left-hand side just before the Kenson Bridge, occupied by the American born Tom Roberts and his young family. We turn to the left over the bridge and at the corner is the Rose and Crown which, after it ceases to be a pub in 1907, will become occupied for many years by the large Bryan family. Proceeding up the steep track of Barren Hill past the cottages, soon to be homes for the Vizard, Regan, Wiltshire and Palmer families, we reach the Mount, that busy "shopping centre". Next door is the Red Cow where the Hopkin family will remain for nearly thirty more years. Arthur Davies, the six foot scar-faced policeman is in the police house with the letter carrier, Joseph Smith next door. There is then open ground which the boys from the school will soon be using as a garden. Holly and Ivy cottages, used by the Catholics in the area are next, with the chapel and the church being the last buildings before Penmark Farm which has been occupied by the Bowen family for fifty years. The ruins of the castle and of the former vicarage lie away behind the church and the farm. Continuing towards Rhoose, we find Higher End on our right hand side. This large property has been occupied by the Thomas family for nearly a century but is destined to be divided into two cottages following the death of Alexander, today's head of the household. One of the cottages will house his daughter, Leonora, until she dies in 1942 and the other will eventually become "Sivey" Evans' shop. There are no more houses along this road so we turn back. Returning through the village, we pass, opposite the church wall, some farm outbuildings on our left which will later be updated by Evan Williams as high quality barns and stables. We pass four more cottages before arriving at the Six Bells where Edward Aubrey has been the landlord for over thirty years. Next on our left is the Croft which is a large property nearly obscuring from our view the newly inscribed date stone

40. *Penmark vicarage c.1900.*

high on the eastern end wall of the school next door. Behind the school is a large thatched cottage soon to be occupied by Mr Blakemore until it is demolished in the middle of the next century. Beyond the school is a courtyard of four cottages attached to William Thomas's wheelright and carpentry business. Passing Rose cottage, we reach the top of "Well Lane" down which everyone goes to draw water at the well and no doubt to pass on the gossip of the day.

INCUMBENTS OF PENMARK

1242	Thomas of Penmark.
1340	Robert Umfreville.
1425	John Dawkyn.
1509	John Pyll.
1534	Richard Lewis.
1540	Sir Thomas ap Lewis ap Rees Lloyd.
1541	Thomas Seyes.
1554	John Seyes.
1555	Richard Eles.
1588	Morgan Blethin M.A.
1590	David Slugge.
1611	Jenkin Mayo M.A.
1623	John Butler.
1662	Edward Morgan M.A.
1678	John Lougher M.A.
1685	John Jenkin M.A. B.D.
1689	Howell William.
1707	Richard Gregory M.A.
1742	Edward Pordage.
1744	Daniel Newcome D.D.
1747	Noah Neale Newcome M.A.
1758	Curates Henry Jones and Rowland Jay.
1783	Henry Jones M.A.
1795	W. Sergrove D.D.
1796	Joseph A.Small D.D.
1799	John Thomas Casberd L.L.D.
1843	Frederick Charles B.Wood M.A.
1891	Edward Morgan. M.A.
1901	Percy Mortimer M.A.
1923	John David Evans.
1933	Thomas Pritchard Price B.A.
1938	William Hubert Harris Williams M.A.
1969	John Frederick Williams B.A.

41 & 42. The Six Bells.

EARLY PARISH COUNCILLORS

O.H. Jones	Chairman 1895-1917
Ed. Morgan	
William James Thomas Jones	
William Rees	
Matthew Evans	
Thomas Harbottle	
Mr Dunscombe	
John Lester	
Mr Alexander	
Thomas Thomas	
James Lougher	Chairman 1917-1928
Thomas James	Chairman 1928-1931
Mr Dunnett	Chairman 1931-1936
Mr Wiltshire	Chairman 1936
John Aubrey	
William Vizard	
John Blakemore	

PARISH CLERK

Thomas Harbottle	1895-1917
Frederick Duck	1917-1924
W.J. Roberts	1924-1936
G. Watkins	1936-1938
W.R. Bassett	1938-1955

43.   *George Hutching school master 1859.*

TEACHERS AT PENMARK SCHOOL WITH PLACE OF BIRTH AND AGES WHEN APPOINTED

Year	Name	Age	Place	Notes
1848	Josia & Ann Taylor	22	Portishead	
1856	Thomas Llewellyn			
1859	George Hutchings	26	Deptford	went to Barry
1861	William Prosser	31	Anglesey	
1864	Walter Thomas			
1865	George Glover			
1867	George Passmore			
1869	Thomas Arthur	47	Staffs	died in May 1877
1877	David Richards	53		died July 1878
1878	Mary Richards	21	Merthyr	
1880	Janetta West	18	Northants	pupil teacher
1883	Emily Jones			assistant
1885	David Richards			
1885	Elizabeth Williams			resigned 1888
1888	Rosa Nurton			resigned 1890
1891	Frederick Duck	21	Abergavenny	resigned 1930
1892	Miss L. Thomas	30		1929
1916	Miss Gregory		Llanbethery	assistant 1925
1925	Miss Crowther			1928
1930	Mr Reese			went to Dinas Powis 1933
1930	Miss Jones			1931
1931	Miss Edmunds			from Porthkerry school